AF890423

NEST EGG CARE

Find Your SAFE SPENDING RATE to Maximize the Joys of Retirement

Know How Much to Spend and How to Invest So You Won't Outlive Your Money

Spend and Gift More in Retirement Than You Ever Thought Possible

Develop Your Retirement Financial Plan

A Workbook by

TOM CANFIELD

Nest Egg Care:
Find Your Safe Spending Rate to Maximize the Joys of Retirement
by Tom Canfield

Copyright © 2017 by Tom Canfield

ISBN: 9780692916223
LCCN: 2017911665

Editor: Evan Pattak
Book Design and Production: Mike Murray, Pearhouse Productions, pearhouse.com

Notice of Rights

All rights reserved. No part of this book may be reproduced or transmitted by any means, electronic, mechanical, photocopying, recording, or otherwise, without the prior written permission of the author. For information on getting permission for reprints and excerpts, contact permissions@nesteggcare.com.

Notice of Liability

The information in this book is distributed on an "As Is" basis, without warranty. While every precaution has been taken in the preparation of the book, the author shall not have any liability to any person or entity with respect to any loss or damage caused or alleged to be caused directly or indirectly by the instructions contained in the book or by the computer software or programs at web sites cited in the book.

This publication is designed to provide accurate and authoritative information in regard to the subject matter covered. It is sold with the understanding that the author is not engaged in rendering legal, accounting, futures/securities trading, or other professional service. If legal advice or other expert assistance is required, the services of a competent professional person should be sought.

Trademarks and Copyrights

Many of the designations use by manufacturers and sellers to distinguish their products are claimed as trademarks. Where those designations appear in this book and the author was aware of a trademark, the author designated the first occurence by ®. All other product names and services identified throughout this book are used in editorial fashion only and for the benefit of such companies with no intention of infringement of the trademark. No such use, or the use of any trade name, is intended to convey endorsement or other affiliation with the book.

Screen shots of displays from Internet web sites (and images redrawn to enhance print quality) from FIRECalc® and Vanguard® are copyrights of their respective owners and are used with permission and identified as requested. Nest Egg Care is a service mark of Nest Egg Care, LLC.

Find us on the web at www.nesteggcare.com

TABLE OF CONTENTS

Resources Available at www.nesteggcare.com

Introduction	Planning Worksheet, similar to Appendix A (.pdf)
Chapter 1	Article: Find your SSR% if you have a large inflow or outflow (.pdf)
Chapter 3	Spreadsheet to create your table of Living and Dying Probabilities, similar to Appendix E (.xlsx)
Chapter 6	Spreadsheet to calculate your current Investing Cost, similar to Appendix F (.xlsx)
Chapter 9	Spreadsheet for your potential SSR% for many future years, similar to Appendix G (.xlsx)
Chapter 9	Spreadsheet for your SSA calculation, similar to Appendix H (.xlsx)
Chapter 9	Display of our Annual SSA Calculation each December (.pdf)
Chapter 13	Spreadsheet to aid in rebalancing your portfolio: rebalance as you withdraw for spending (.xlsx)

■ ■ ■

Dedication

I remember my Dad reading the financial pages, looking to find what happened that day to stocks he owned. I wondered what that was all about. Dad, I think I learned more than a little.

My Mom could solve word and math puzzles in a flash. Ones that took me days to solve would take her minutes. Mom, this one was a puzzle I really enjoyed working on.

Thank you, Patti. Collaborator. Tolerator. Most fun person. Ever.

INTRODUCTION

Why I Wrote This Book

INTRODUCTION

Why I Wrote This Book

Now that you're retired or approaching retirement, you may find yourself thinking differently about the future. If you're like me, your thinking can be boiled down to a single question: Will we outlive and outspend the money we worked so hard to save and invest?

You've spent decades to build your nest egg — you played that game successfully. Now, though, you're a player in a different game. You have monthly Social Security income and perhaps other retirement income to spend. But the cash you take from your portfolio is likely the largest source of your "monthly paycheck." Deciding on 1) how much cash to meter out for spending and gifting, and 2) how to invest wisely are very different tasks than you've faced before.

If you're retired or a few years away from retirement, you should make these two key decisions NOW. Even if retirement is many years away, you may want to think about these choices so that you'll have a much better idea of how much you should save and how you should invest.

My wife, Patti, and I have been savers and investors for years. I thought the assets we'd accumulated would be "enough" for whatever the future might bring. Yet Patti's questions about our spending — "Can we really afford this hotel room?" "Do we have enough to afford the things we like to do?" — while legitimate enough, were little pinpricks to my sense of security. I realized that I didn't really know if we had enough. So to give us a comfort level about our spending, to assure as best one can that our savings would fund the life we want, I set about finding out.

I started to formulate our plan in fall 2014 and implemented it a few months later. For starters, I wrote down these key questions:

- *Do we have enough?* What can we spend? Or, if we know what we'd like to spend, how much do we need?

- *How should we invest?* In which specific mutual funds should we invest? What's the proper mix of stocks and bonds for us? What do we do when market returns dive?
- *Might we have more than enough in the future?* How would we know? How much more might we be able to spend or gift to those we care about while we're alive?

As basic and important as these questions are, trying to answer them proved frustrating. I encountered a number of rules of thumb — such as the "Four Percent Rule" (a rule of thumb as to how much you can spend per year in retirement)[1] — that were too general for me. I interviewed financial advisors in search of more specifics, but they couldn't give me better answers than the rules of thumb. Weeks into my research, I was all thumbs and no answers.

Thus, I decided to dig in and figure it out myself. I found some excellent — and free, believe it or not — tools on the Internet that helped me determine the answers to our questions. Now, Patti and I know what the tools tell us we can safely spend, and we understand the simple investing rules that those tools tell us we must follow.

Four factors determine if you will outspend and outlive your money: 1) how much of your savings you spend; 2) how you invest; 3) the pattern of future returns you'll face; and 4) your life span. In that equation, you decide the first two; you don't control the last two uncertainties.

Patti and Tom, Summer 2015

I wrote this book so you can sweep the fear of the apocalypse of outspending and outliving your nest egg off the table. You will know how to avoid grave mistakes of spending too much or investing incorrectly. You will find your Safe Spending Rate that squarely faces the uncertainties of future returns and life span. You'll virtually have no chance of running out of money – even in the face of horrible future financial returns.

Another reason for this book: to help you maximize the joys of retirement. We're all victims of not knowing what's safe to spend and how to invest. I maintain that we're unnecessarily punishing ourselves in retirement. We fall into the default financial plan that minimizes our worry and that we judge best meets our responsibilities as parents and grandparents: spend and give less now, invest super-conservatively, and hope that our portfolio remains steady and grows for enough bequests after we're gone.

Your retirement can be much better. You can enjoy more now and in the future. Once you know the facts, you'll likely find your Safe Spending Amount is more than you think, and, if you are retired, is more than you are spending now. Patti and I found we clearly can start our plan by spending more than the Four Percent Rule would impose, for example. And the better news is that it's almost certain your Safe Spending Amount will be greater in a few years: you can both spend and gift more over the rest of your lives – perhaps twice as much as you thought possible – with no greater risk than you feel you're taking now.

One implementation task has been key in changing our thinking about how we'll spend our remaining years: since we're confident in the amount we have calculated as safe to spend each year, we "pay ourselves" that amount during the year, and we know we don't have to save one dime of it. And we don't. Instead, our focus has changed: "What's the next fun thing we should do?" And, typically, later in each year we ask, "Who should benefit from our increased giving this year? And how much?" I hope you think about spending your remaining years similarly because one thing is certain: you'll enjoy your retirement more when you give to your loved ones and/or your favorite causes while you're still around to appreciate the impact you've made.

Is This Book for You?

This book won't be for everyone. Going through this process challenged my intuition and "common sense" advice I've read about how much to spend and how to invest. Some folks have been retired for years, and their patterns of spending and investing are fixed in their minds. If you're among them – which is to say your beliefs are unshakable – this book is not for you. Here are a few points that could jangle your beliefs or thought processes:

- Your real worry-point is many years away — typically decades. I've heard people say, "Forget 20 years from now. Stock returns are off 5% *this* year, and I'm frightened." This fear seems unshakable; the overarching priority of these folks is lowest possible variability in their portfolio value over time. *Next Egg Care* focuses on the risk of depleting your portfolio far out into the future. It acknowledges the reality that we'll almost certainly experience "bad variability" in annual returns for stocks and bonds in the upcoming decades. This book tells you what to do to survive a panic attack. But if you think you can't work through "bad variability" when it inevitably strikes – even when armed with survival tactics – this book is not for you.

✦ The Safe Spending Rate you will calculate from this book is always greater than the stated percentage that the IRS requires you to withdraw from your retirement accounts starting at age 70½. (I refer to the amount calculated as MRD – the minimum required distribution.) And your Safe Spending Amount is always much more than your MRD. I've had people tell me, "I just take my MRD, along with Social Security, and that's what we live off. We're happy and don't need to spend more." Well, that's fine, and I'd judge that amount they spend is perfectly safe — even if they violate the investing rules proposed in this book. In my opinion, though, those folks could be safely enjoying so much more. If you're perfectly happy and have no interest in spending or gifting more during your lifetime than you do now, this book is not for you.

✦ You'll almost certainly have More-Than-Enough in the future. For example, it's almost certain that you won't ride one of those horrible sequences of returns that drives your initial Safe Spending Rate (and spending amount) to a low level. I've heard people say, "There is no such thing as More-Than-Enough." *Nest Egg Care* challenges that belief and will ask you to calculate frequently to determine if you have More-Than-Enough and, when you do, the book also asks, "Now what do you do?" If you're firm in your belief that there's no such thing as More-Than-Enough, this book is not for you.

✦ A lower mix of stocks relative to bonds buys you little and potentially "hurts" you more over your long, long retirement period. This one really rocks conventional wisdom and our intuition. The fact is that a lower mix of stocks is a minor contributor to lowering the probability of depleting a portfolio, but a lower mix has an outsized effect of reducing your probable future portfolio value. Armed with these details, choosing your mix of stocks is easy, but it's different than most people think. If you're happy with the low mix of stocks you now have in your portfolio, the facts presented in *Nest Egg Care* will make you uncomfortable to the point that, really, this book is not for you.

✦ Performing no work is better than performing hard work. This notion goes

> against what we've done our whole lives and how we think about ourselves. We view ourselves as competitive. We're smart. We've worked hard. We're above average. We think we can invest our retirement savings and beat the market or that we can select some guru who will invest for us and beat the market. *Nest Egg Care* argues that attempting to beat the market is a fool's errand. Successful investing is shockingly simple. If you're devoted to fiddling with your portfolio in search of ways to beat the market, this book is not for you.

If your beliefs are not unshakable, and you want to learn how to have a better financial plan than you do now, then read on. You're in for a pleasant – and reassuring – surprise.

Drilling Down to the CORE

If we think of retirement as a sport or game, we win that game by playing (spending) very safely, always assuming very poor game conditions in the future. We'll play better by following the right game tactics (how we invest), which will keep us in the bounds of safety. Oddly enough, the right game tactics mean it's very likely we could have much more fun (spend much more) for our whole game.

I've captured this approach in what I think of as four CORE principles: Choose, Obey, Recalculate, Execute. **Choose** your Safe Spending Rate (SSR%). **Obey** the Rules of the Game. **Recalculate**: It can only get better. **Execute** and keep it simple. I've organized this book into those four parts; I'll introduce the principles now but elaborate in later chapters.

A central theme runs through these CORE principles, one usually not emphasized or even discussed in many articles on retirement planning. That theme is the first key rule of the game that you must **Obey:** you *must* be a low-cost investor and match as closely as you can future "market returns" for stocks and bonds. You will reliably be low cost if you invest in Index Funds that track the broad stock and bond markets. All other decisions you make are much clearer if you commit to being low cost; they're muddled if you don't. If you're low cost, your ability to **Choose** a safe spending rate is straightforward. You can confidently **Recalculate** when and how much more you can spend in the future. Your plan becomes very simple to **Execute**.

Here's a short overview.

1. Choose your Safe Spending Rate (SSR%).

Your SSR% is a constant-dollar (C$) amount of spending (the numerator) per $1 million Starting Portfolio value (the denominator). That constant-dollar amount adjusts for inflation to maintain its same purchasing power over time independent of the variations in investment returns. (In **Recalculate,** we find the amount you can spend most likely will increase by more than inflation in the future.) In simple terms, your SSR% determines the amount you can spend from your nest egg in a given year without jeopardizing the long-term health of your savings.

How do we calculate our SSR%? First, we'll use a tool called a Retirement Withdrawal Calculator (RWC) to tell us how a portfolio fares for a given spending rate over the wide range of the possible sequences of future stock and bond returns. To determine our SSR%, we focus on the horrible sequences of returns. Each spending rate has a number of years of zero probability of depleting a portfolio and a rising probability of depletion thereafter.

Next, we deploy a tool called a Probability of Living Calculator to help us get a good idea on the probable length of our game and the Safe Spending Rate (SSR%) that is safe over our lifetime. The SSR% you pick will be safe in horrible patterns over many years, with essentially zero chances of depleting your portfolio for typically decades and very low chances (about 1-in-50) in the years thereafter.

The SSR% you pick is age dependent. Younger folks will expect their game to be longer. They'll want more years of zero chance of depleting their portfolio; their SSR% will be lower. If you're older, your SSR% is greater; you won't need your money for as many years, so you can safely spend more. For once, older is better. Patti and I chose 4.40% as our initial SSR%, which translates to C$44,000 per $1 million starting Investment Portfolio.

Finally, you'll use your SSR% to find your initial Safe Spending Amount (SSA) — that was the multiplication of our $44,000 per $1 million starting portfolio times our "Multiplier," which is our Investment Portfolio divided by $1 million. Or, you can use the inverse of the rate (that is 22.7 in our case) as a multiplier to tell you how much Investment Portfolio you need for a desired constant-dollar level of spending.

2. Obey the Rules of the Game: You must obey two key rules, and the first one is critical.

RULE #1: YOU MUST BE A LOW-COST INVESTOR. All the RWCs that help find your Safe Spending Rate are based on the assumption that you match or very nearly match "market returns" for stocks and bonds. We all incur costs when we invest, and the tool we use to find a Safe Spending Rate deducts these costs from a portfolio along with the withdrawal for spending for the upcoming year.

When you invest in Index Funds, you are predictably low cost relative to "market returns" — as low as 0.05% Investing Cost per year deducted from your Investment Portfolio. Index funds return about 97% of "market returns" to investors.

However, when you invest in Actively Managed Funds, you are not predictably low cost. The cost of the average Actively Managed Fund was about 1.20% per year in 2015. In aggregate, Actively Managed Funds must mathematically underperform index funds exactly by their higher costs, and they do. Actively Managed Funds return about 88% of market returns to investors.

Each year some Actively Managed Funds *do* beat their peer index fund; they can outperform only because other Actively Managed Funds have very badly underperformed. It's not the same funds that beat their peer index year after year. It's a vanishing, small probability that you or someone you pay can pick Actively Managed Funds that overcome their higher costs over the long haul to result in lower net cost than Index Funds.

RULE #2: TUCK AWAY 5% OF YOUR PORTFOLIO AS AN OFF-THE-TOP RESERVE. This Reserve is your hedge when you're hit with "bad variability" of returns. Keep your Reserve separate from the rest. Remember that when you do this, you're applying your SSR% to the remaining 95%, your Investment Portfolio.

Your SSR% is calculated to be safe even in the face of horrible sequences of future returns. But when I look in detail at those bad sequences, I know they would shake my sense of feeling worry free. The bad ones are *really* bad, typically hitting hard right at the start of a retirement period.

We'll all be socked with "bad variability" of returns sometime during our retirement. I define "bad variability" as a bad 1-in-10-year event; statistically, that's a year of real stock returns of -17% or worse. It's 90% probable that we'll see at least one year like that in the next 20. We all hope that doesn't befall us right off the bat or for at least several years after we've started our game. When you're first hit, though, you'll tap the Reserve, not your Investment Portfolio. Plan on refilling the Reserve when stocks rebound.

You'll also make your choice of stocks/bonds mix in this part of the book. A lower mix of stocks turns out to be a minor contributor to lowering the probability of depleting a portfolio for any spending rate. I was surprised to find that; I think most retirees would share my surprise. A lower stock mix also slashes your potential portfolio balance over your long, long game. Given those two points, the choice of mix becomes very clear.

3. Recalculate: It can only be good news.

When your returns are not on a horrible path, you will accumulate more than you need for your current Safe Spending Amount, and therefore you can spend more. You can calculate if you have More-Than-Enough and how much more you can spend. You can expect — if the sequence of future returns you ride along is an average one — to be able to spend about twice your initial Safe Spending Amount.

I suggest you recalculate no less frequently than every three years, but you could do it more often. I recalculate annually, and after the first two years, we're now spending, relative to our initial $1 million starting Investment Portfolio, $46,100 in 2017. That's a 4.5% real increase from our initial $44,000.

When you accumulate More-Than-Enough, you'll be faced with the question: what do we really gain by holding onto this "excess"? Patti and I decided to gift the excess now to those we care about rather than waiting to get it to them after we're gone. That's given us a sense of meaning and joy that I think we otherwise would not have.

4. Execute: Keep it simple.

It's easy to be an effective, low-cost investor. You need to invest in only three or four broad-based Index Funds. Your choices are simple and basically unchanging over time. Based on history, you'll be in the top 10% or so of all investors over time.

But this simplicity goes against well-known behaviors and biases we all have. The hardest challenge for me is to resist the urge to fiddle with my portfolio. Our human bias is to act to control the future, and fiddling gives us the illusion of control. It's hard to accept that we will win our game with just a few mutual funds and no time spent changing them.

It takes time to initially re-orient your portfolio to just a few index funds and to set up your Reserve account. You'll want your Investment Portfolio all in one place (brokerage house), and you'll want to organize your accounts such that you and your spouse/partner can easily see and understand the total picture.

Year-end maintenance tasks are straightforward, but they require a good checklist and a couple of spreadsheets to help you calculate your SSA and rebalance your portfolio. You'll find useful spreadsheets at this book's companion Web site, **www.nesteggcare.com**. As you gain experience with the methodology, you'll reduce the time spent on maintenance tasks to just a few hours at the end of each year.

You have a Worksheet that will document your decisions

Appendix A is Your Plan Worksheet you will complete as you go through this book. It's short and sweet. You can download and print a copy at **www.nesteggcare.com.**

Appendix B shows our design choices when we started our plan in December 2014 and our schedule of maintenance tasks. I'm able to compress our Worksheet down to a 3x5 card that I've taped to the side of my computer screen as shown on the right (reduced).

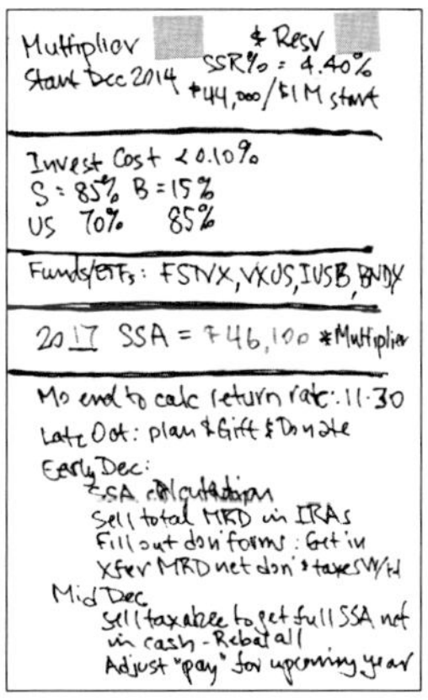

You'll find much more detail on the four CORE principles

in the following pages. I'm confident you'll find them easy to understand and implement. To help in that regard, I've included a list of "action items" for you at the close of each section. You'll also find "The Patti & Tom File," a look at how we applied the CORE approach and how it's played out for us. The bottom line: it's enabled us to spend and gift more now while remaining confident in the solidity of our portfolio.

This ACTION STEP symbol, seen throughout the book, is your cue to head to the Appendix pages or our website as specified.

■ ■ ■

To get you started with something fun, I've constructed the self-test below. Full disclosure: had I taken this test in the fall of 2014 before I formalized our plan, I would have scored poorly. My design choices would have been mere guesses. I had not even thought of Investing Cost as a design choice. (It is.) I particularly did not understand the interplay of these four design factors. Patti and I both clearly understand now. When you're finished with this book, you'll have the specifics, and your total score should be 20.

SELF-TEST: CONFIDENCE LEVEL IN YOUR CHOICES

DESIGN CHOICES	Not at all Confident 0	Totally Confident 5	Your Score
A Safe Spending Rate, % See note.			
B Mix: Stocks and Bonds Percentages			
C Weight: US and International Percentages			
D Gross Investing Cost, % See note.			
		Sum	

RANK A, B, C, and D in Importance ☐ ☐ ☐ ☐

A Annual constant $ spending rate. A simple way to look at this: Do you know what percent could you safely spend from your portfolio in the next 12 months?

D Gross Investing Costs you incur: Weighted Expense Ratio of all funds you own + Advisory Fees as a percentage of total portfolio value

PART 1

Choose Your Initial SAFE SPENDING RATE

- CHAPTER 1 -

AT THE STARTING GATE: DEFINE YOUR FINANCIAL PORTFOLIO

IN THIS CHAPTER...

* Add up your financial portfolio at the start of your plan.
* This book assumes that's a simple task.
* Your tasks may be more complex:
  - If you find yourself home equity rich and financial assets poor
  - If you have significant future inflows or outflows to your financial portfolio.

Start the process of planning by defining your financial portfolio and enter your total on Your Plan Worksheet (Appendix A.). This table shows how I think about it:

OUR NEST EGG (THE TOTAL)

A Checking Accounts /Savings Accnts	$
B Investment Accounts	
Taxable	$
Retirement/Tax Deferred	$
Subtotal: Financial Assets (A+B)	$
Home Equity (est.)	$
Other Non-Financial Assets	
Real Estate and other (net)	na
Stuff: cars, furnishings, Patti's shoes	$ 0
Subtotal Non-Financial Assets	$
Total Net Assets:	$

That's our focus

Exclude your home and all other non-financial assets that you don't want to convert into cash for spending. I'm assuming in this book that your financial assets far outweigh the equity in your home. At this time of life, we want to maximize our financial assets and capacity. We certainly don't want to be home equity rich and cash poor.

You may judge that, indeed, you *are* home equity (and non-financial asset) rich and financial assets poor. If that's the case, I recommend you consider a mortgage (if you don't have one), a home equity line of credit or a reverse mortgage to free your "pent-up" cash.

I've always had a home mortgage and always will. Therefore, our non-cash asset of home equity is modest relative to our financial assets. I last refinanced and increased our mortgage in late 2012 when mortgage interest rates were rock bottom, close to 3% for a 30-year mortgage. In years past, my logic was that the cost of my loan (after the tax deduction for interest expense and the effect of inflation) was always less than about 2% real cost per year, and I thought that for the 30 years that I held a portion of that money, I likely would earn +6% real return, which is the average return rate for stocks. I'd always come out ahead. That's still true today, especially on the rock-bottom interest rate I pay, but it's pretty clear I won't be around in 30 years. The main advantage now that we're retired is to have the cash that's now invested to provide us a real future return and flexibility to spend. It isn't to "make more money" (although that's almost certain to be true).

I also obtained the largest home equity line of credit I could at the start of our plan. It costs nothing but time to obtain and maintain it. I don't envision any major home repairs and never expect to use it, but that instant borrowing power just adds to our financial capacity. In case of an emergency I can draw on that line immediately. (That line of credit is in addition to the essentially cash Reserve I describe in Chapter 7.)

My neighbor, Hal, died about three years ago. His wife, Alice, continues to live in the home they bought in 1975. Today, it's worth about $450,000, and she has no mortgage. Alice has about $1 million in financial assets. To me, $450,000 is far too much to tie up in an asset that provides no cash to spend — and requires cash just to maintain it.

I talked to Alice about the fact that almost one-third of her net worth is tied up in her house. She doesn't like the idea of a mortgage or reverse mortgage, but she's okay with getting the largest home equity line of credit she can get. She also knows she has some home maintenance and improvements to undertake, so in my mind, using the home equity loan for those purposes makes sense. Whatever she spends is either maintaining or enhancing the value of her home.

Your financial assets provide you the cash to enjoy, so I'd advise not spending that money on replacing the stucco, unless you really fancy stucco! So, yes, Alice should remodel the second floor bathroom to make it more elder-accessible. She should install a small washer and drier somewhere on that floor so she's not carrying laundry up and down two flights of stairs. But use the home equity line of credit for that. Her bank gave her a $290,000 line of credit! She'll never remotely get close to using that, but I think that over time, that added financial capacity will ease her worries about the future.

I also suggested that Alice consider paying her property taxes and home owner's insurance from her home equity line; her home will likely increase in value by at least 2% per year ($9,000), and those two payments add up to less than that. We'll see if she acts on that next January.

Determining our total portfolio was straightforward for Patti and me. We had "right-sized" our home a decade ago. We have no investments in other real estate that could reduce our financial resources. We'll have no potential large cash inflows or outflows to/from our financial portfolio that would make our situation more complex: no future inheritances, no future proceeds from insurance for a surviving spouse.

Your situation may be more complex than ours. If you expect a large future inflow, for example, your initial Safe Spending Rate would be greater than you would derive from the process described in this book. I suggest how to solve a more complex situation in an article you can download from the Web site: **www.nesteggcare.com**.

■ ■ ■

Calculate your "Investment Portfolio" on Your Plan Worksheet — that's 95% of the total, since 5% is a Reserve. I'll discuss the need for a Reserve in Part 2. This Reserve is Off-the-Top. It's not part of your thinking to determine how much your can safely spend in a year. Your Investment Portfolio is the resource that will fund your spending. You'll apply your Safe Spending Rate (SSR%) to your Investment Portfolio (the 95%) to get to your annual Safe Spending Amount (SSA). But you won't use your total portfolio in this calculation.

Divide your starting Investment Portfolio by $1 million to get your "Multiplier."

I state many results in this book in terms of spending amounts per $1 million starting Investment Portfolio. You'll use your Multiplier for the calculations to get your total annual Safe Spending Amount. And you'll use this same "Multiplier" in future years to get to your "More-Than-Enough" amount that I discuss in Part 3.

SUMMARY At the start of your planning process, add up your financial portfolio and do some simple math to get to what this book describes as your Investment Portfolio and Multiplier. Don't count your home equity or other non-financial assets as part of your financial portfolio, and I assume in this book that you are not home equity rich and financial resources poor. You have some choices to make if you are. In any case, I recommend you obtain the largest home equity line of credit that you can; even if you never use it, it will add to your financial capacity and sense of well-being.

- CHAPTER 2 -

The Probability That a Spending Rate Depletes a Portfolio

IN THIS CHAPTER...

- ★ Retirement Withdrawal Calculators ▸▸ Data for Probability Depleting a Portfolio
- ★ Each Spending Rate ▸▸ Unique Curve of the Year-by-Year Probabilities
- ★ Probability Curves Look Like Hockey Sticks:
  - Many years of zero chances of depleting (stick shaft);
  - Rising chances thereafter (blade angle).
- ★ We can display Years of Zero Probability of Depleting vs. Spending Rate

We retired folks are acutely aware that we face uncertain future investment returns. The long-run historical return rate for stocks is 6.4% real return per year, and it's 2.6% for bonds.[1] If annual returns rates were steady, our task would be easy: invest 100% in stocks. But return rates aren't steady, and that's what makes our task not so easy.

Both stocks and bonds have varied widely from those long-run average rates for all holding periods. (A "holding period" is how long you hold an investment before you sell it.) The return rates for stocks are three times more variable than bonds for a one-year holding period. That difference in variation narrows as the holding period lengthens, but in the past, we have experienced long periods of essentially zero percent cumulative returns for both stocks and bonds. Fortunately, stocks and bonds weren't lock-step in those periods: bonds often zigged when stocks zagged.[2]

We just don't know now what pattern or sequence of annual returns we'll experience in retirement. Will we see one of those substandard sequences of returns, an average sequence of returns, or a better-than-average sequence of returns? We plan very conservatively, always assuming we'll face horrible sequences of returns, and that assumption drives a spending rate that does not deplete a portfolio to low levels.

We start our planning by understanding the year-by-year probabilities of outspending and therefore depleting our portfolio. This is pretty obvious: the more you spend from your portfolio, the greater the probability that you'll deplete your portfolio in a future year.

We calculate the probabilities of depleting a portfolio for a spending rate that is a constant-dollar (C$) spending amount (the numerator) per $1 million Starting Portfolio value (the denominator). Constant-dollar spending amount means the money you withdraw from your portfolio for spending retains its same purchasing power over time; the dollar amount adjusts each year for inflation similar to the way Social Security adjusts each year. That C$ amount stays the same independent of the value of your portfolio until a recalculation tells us we can increase it (See Part 3). Spending is pre-tax, meaning you have to pay your income taxes out of that amount. I discuss some tactics to keep taxes low in Chapters 10 and 13.

Your **Safe Spending Rate (SSR%)** is the rate you pick that results in no chance of depleting a portfolio for many years — typically decades — and very low chances of depleting your portfolio for the years thereafter.

Let's note that "depleting your portfolio" is not the same as "going broke." In addition to what you spend from your Investment Portfolio, you'll have Social Security and perhaps other retirement income that always will be there for you to spend. As mentioned in Chapter 1, we did not include non-financial assets, such as your home equity, as part of your financial portfolio; those assets are a deep, deep reserve.

■ ■ ■

We use a Retirement Withdrawal Calculator (RWC) to give us data for the year-by-year probability that a spending rate depletes a portfolio. If you search the Internet for "retirement withdrawal calculator," you'll get over 400,000 results. I reviewed all on the first eight pages of results; that alone amounted to more than 100 RCWs. Most of them really are no help in understanding the future probability of depleting a portfolio because they rely on one steady, average rate of return for all future years.

We want to use the kind of RWC that recognizes the variability in the sequences in annual returns we may face. These RWCs construct many year-by-year sequences of stock and bond returns that represent the complete range we might experience. Each sequence they build is different and could range from the worst ever in history to the best.

For a given spending amount, an RWC tracks how a Starting Portfolio fares year-by-year for each sequence of annual returns it constructs. We first input a mix of stocks and bonds, and the RWC builds many sequences of returns from its store of returns rates. We then input a beginning portfolio value (I always pick $1 million.) and a constant-dollar spending amount. Using $1 million as our starting portfolio value makes the calculation of the rate simple: spending of C$44,000 per year is 4.40% spending rate, for example.

Now, the RWC is ready to calculate. It picks its first sequence of returns. It subtracts an initial withdrawal for spending in the first year, maintaining the chosen mix of stocks and bonds. It then applies the return rate for the first year to obtain a new balance at the end of the first year. Next, it subtracts next year's spending (and may also subtract Investing Costs incurred in the year) and rebalances the portfolio to the chosen mix of stocks and bonds. Then it repeats the steps year-by-year for as many future years as you desire. And then it performs the same steps on another sequence.

At the end of a year, if there is enough to take a withdrawal for spending for the next year, the RWC counts that sequence as "successful." If the portfolio balance has declined to the point that it does not allow a full withdrawal for spending, the RWC counts that sequence as a "failure." For each year, the RWC counts the number of sequences that succeed and the ones that fail.

The RWC expresses the percent that are successful as a "success rate," "probability that your portfolio survives," or similar term. We're focused on understanding the chances of depleting our portfolio. We get to the "probability of depleting" as 100% minus the "success rate."

■ ■ ■

In Graph 2-1, you can see how a starting portfolio changed year-by-year for one spending level and for just three sequences of returns that one RWC assembled. Both spending and portfolio values are in constant dollars. This graph shows us how year-end portfolio value changed as it marched along each of the three sequences for about 30 years.

GRAPH 2-1
YEAR-BY-YEAR PORTFOLIO VALUE FOR ONE SPENDING AMOUNT USING A THREE-SEQUENCE CALCULATOR

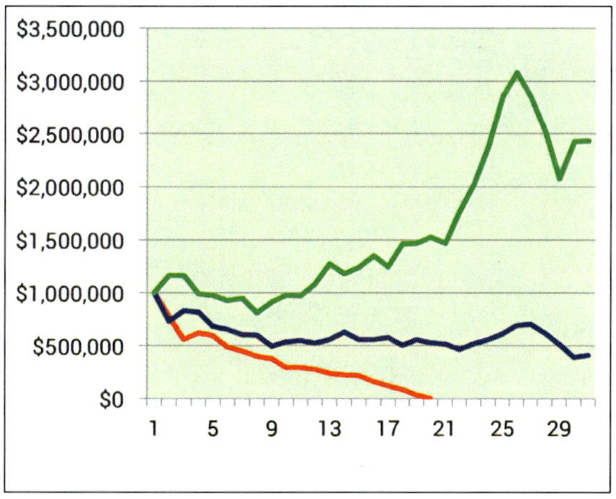

Source: FIRECalc.com

We can envision each sequence of returns as one game condition we may face in the future. In this example the starting portfolio depleted in 19 years as it followed one scenario (red): bad game conditions. The portfolio more than doubled in real spending power at the end of 30 years on another scenario (green): great game conditions. The much greater portfolio value in the future means we could have spent much more during retirement. Or, if we never changed the spending amount as assumed for this graph, we'd accumulate more than twice the starting portfolio amount.

For this three-sequence calculator, we'd count in each year the number of sequences where the portfolio balance did not support a full withdrawal for spending in the next year. We can see that no sequence depleted for the first 19 years, and that one of the three depleted in all subsequent years. We can state that as 0% probability of depleting for 19 years and thereafter a 33% probability of depleting, as depicted in Graph 2-2. We'll see this simple picture repeat: many years of zero probability of failure, an inflection point, and a level of failure thereafter.

GRAPH 2-2
PROBABILITY OF DEPLETING A PORTFOLIO
FROM THREE-SEQUENCE CALCULATOR

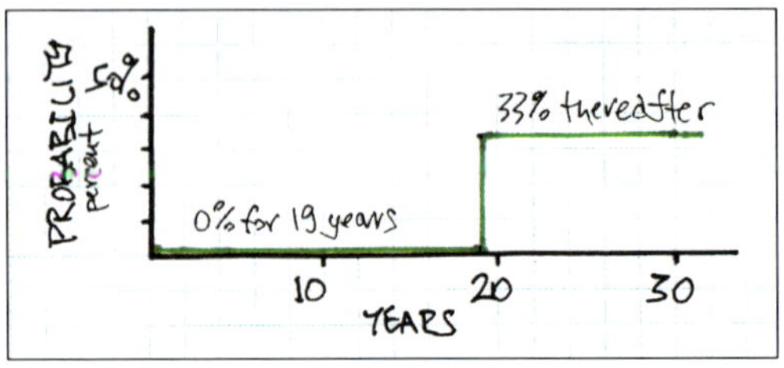

Unfortunately, no RWC lets us input a spending rate (and other parameters) and then draws a probability of depleting curve. I don't know why they don't, but that's the way it is. We can get the data of year-by-year probability of depleting as I did for that three-sequence calculator, but we then must manually plot the data the RWC provides.

■ ■ ■

I found only two RWCs that even give us the data of year-by-year "success rate" so that we can draw a probability of depleting curve. To find only two was amazing to me. Most of the RWCs that properly build many sequences of returns you might face give you their qualitative summary of your planned spending and mix of stocks and bonds, such as "On Track" or "Not on Track," without clearly telling you what the criteria were. The two calculators that give us the data we want are **FIRECalc**® and the **Vanguard**® **Nest Egg Calculator**. Both are excellent, easy to use and provide helpful visual displays, as depicted in Graph 2-3.

GRAPH 2-3
SAMPLE DISPLAY OF RESULTS GRAPH FROM FIRECALC & VANGUARD RWCS

© The Vanguard Group, Inc., used with permission

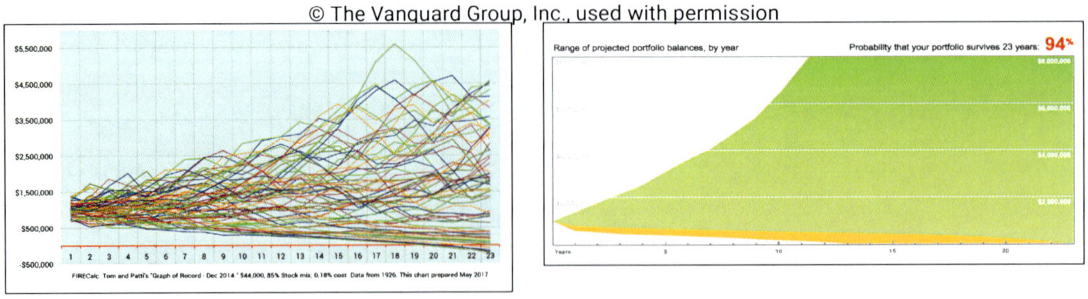

LIST:

FIRECALC RWC: **www.firecalc.com**
VANGUARD RWC:
https://retirementplans.vanguard.com/VGApp/pe/pubeducation/calculators/RetirementNestEggCalc.jsf

I use FIRECalc as the workhorse calculator in this book. FIRECalc gives us information that other calculators don't: we can see clearly how our portfolio fares year-by-year on all sequences of returns; we can see the effect of higher Investing Cost (the cost relative to market returns we incur when we buy and hold securities in our portfolio); we can understand the effect of varying annual spending during retirement. What makes FIRECalc so helpful, though, is that we can understand how each of three inputs (spending rate, Investing Cost, mix of stocks and bonds) affects both the probability of depleting and probable future portfolio value. No other calculator lets us do all that. I use the Vanguard Nest Egg Calculator to verify the key results from FIRECalc.

When we plot the data, we get a probability of depleting curve. FIRECalc and Vanguard both give very similar, but not identical, year-by-year probabilities of depleting a portfolio. Their curves are slightly different. I view them as two manufacturers of probability of depleting curves: they differ in their design philosophy and manufacturing processes. (I personally like FIRECalc's design approach better.) FIRECalc's curves have a long number of years of zero probability of failure, a clear inflection point and a reasonably steep rising probability of failure for the years thereafter. Vanguard curves have a slight curvature before the inflection point that FIRECalc identifies, but after that point, the rising curve is a bit shallower.

We shouldn't obsess over the differences in the two. Both led to the same Safe Spending Rate for Patti and me, and both would lead to the same SSR% for you. Appendix C describes the workings of the FIRECalc and Vanguard RWCs in more detail and how I use them in this book.

■ ■ ■

A picture is worth a thousand words. That's why I love Graph 2-4, taken from FIRECalc's results page. This graph is for 4.40% SSR%: $44,000 in constant-dollar spending per $1 million starting portfolio. Portfolio values are also in constant dollars. I arbitrarily picked 23 years as the end-year of this graph. As you will see later, this is our "Graph of Record" at the start of our plan.

GRAPH 2-4

$44,000 Spending at Our chosen Mix & Investing Cost

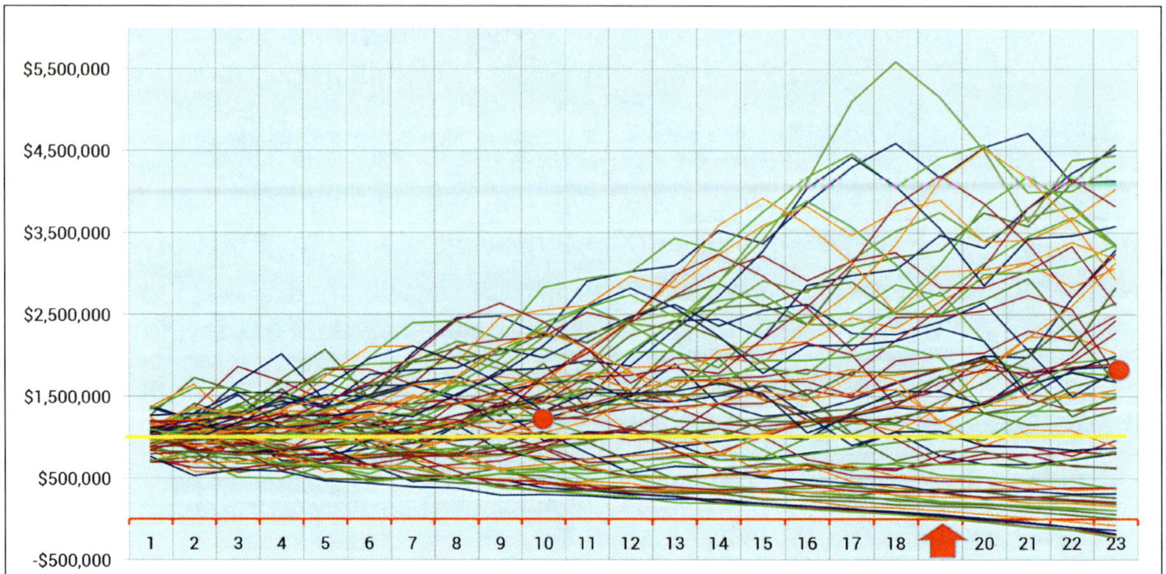

FIRECalc. Tom and Patti's "Graph of Record - Dec 2014." $44,000, 85% Stock mix; 0.18% cost. Data from 1926. This chart prepared May 2017.

I produced this and other graphs you would find on the FIRECalc web site from the actual data. That results in a higher image quality for printing. My colors, sizing, and labels won't exactly match the one you'd see at the web site for the same inputs.

I think I've stared at graphs like this for hours. They tell us a valuable story. You can see the red line for $0. I've added a red arrow, two red dots and a yellow line to help with the narrative.

- We see many possible sequences of returns, and we see how portfolio value changes year-by-year for each sequence. We can see ups and downs; we'll experience good and bad annual returns in the future.
- We see a range of portfolio values for each year; the range widens with more years. It widens more toward greater portfolio value than to less.
- We can see that no sequence depleted for the first 19 years (did not cross the red line; see red arrow), meaning our real point of worry is after 19 years.
- As we look at the 20th year, it appears that a couple of sequences deplete. A few more fail in the following years, and so on. The percentage that have depleted is increasing with more years. At the 23-year mark, the text on the results page for this graph tells us the portfolio depleted in 7% of the

sequences. (The Vanguard calculator indicates that 8% depleted for these same inputs.)

- We see the slope of the lines leading up to depletion. We can roughly trace back the ones that deplete (My eyes most easily can trace back a blue line.), and we get the idea that the sequences that depleted started out badly; we'd have a good idea many years in advance if we were riding a very poor sequence of returns.
- At the 23-year mark, we clearly see that most sequences don't come close to depleting a Starting Portfolio. The text for this graph tells us that the average of all those endpoints is more than $1.7 million; I did my best to place that red dot correctly at the $1.7 million mark. If we experienced the average of the sequence of returns, we'd start with C$1 million, spend over C$1 million (C$44,000 per year for 23 years), and have 70% more in original spending power than we started with! This obviously means we could have increased spending sometime during retirement.
- We also can estimate (by counting as best I can) that about 60% of the endpoints were $1 million or greater. That's the yellow line on the graph. Again, we start with $1 million. We spend more than $1 million, and we have 60% probability that we still have at least $1 million at the end.
- Further, we see that if we are in the middle of the pack, at 10 years, say, none of the lines dive south and heads to failure. I placed a second red dot at roughly the average 10-year value. We get the idea that something's different if our return pattern is not horrible for a few years.

We'll ride one of those sequences of returns in the future, in essence. We just don't know which one at the start of our game. We launch our plan by focusing on the horrible sequences, those few that cross that red line at the bottom of the graph. Those are the scenarios that drive our initial Safe Spending Rate to a low level.

■ ■ ■

Each spending rate has its own year-by-year probability of depleting a portfolio. When I graph the FIRECalc data for a spending rate, the curve looks like a hockey stick when laid out on a graph: the many years of zero probability of failure comprise the shaft, and the rising probability of failure thereafter is the blade angle. I like to think of the curves as physical hockey sticks and describe them by the spending amount per $1 million starting portfolio. The probability curve for a 3.50% spending rate is a $35,000 hockey stick, for example.

The $35,000 stick shown in Graph 2-5 has a very long shaft and a shallow blade angle. It's best for long games, typically 30 or more years. A long game means less spending, and we play our game more slowly and cautiously. **Longer Shaft = Less Spending**.

GRAPH 2-5
3.50% OR $35,000 HOCKEY STICK.
LONG SHAFT. SHALLOW BLADE ANGLE.

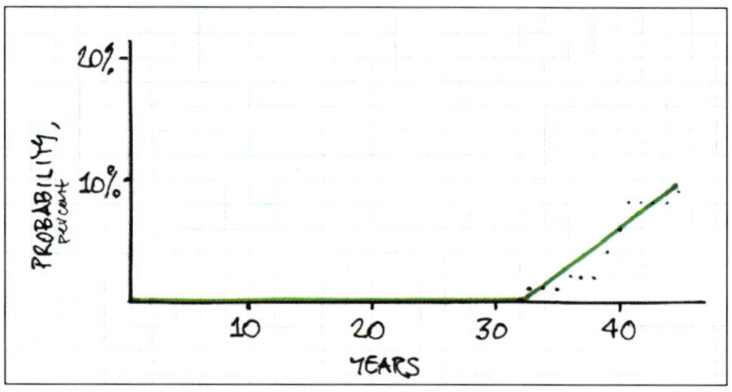

FIRECalc brand and its default assumptions

The $75,000 stick has a short shaft and a steep blade angle. It looks almost like a scythe. It's best for a short game, typically less than 10 years or so. A short game means more spending, and we can play faster and have more fun with this stick. **Shorter Shaft = Greater Spending.**

GRAPH 2-6
7.50% OR $75,000 HOCKEY STICK.
SHORT SHAFT. STEEP BLADE ANGLE.

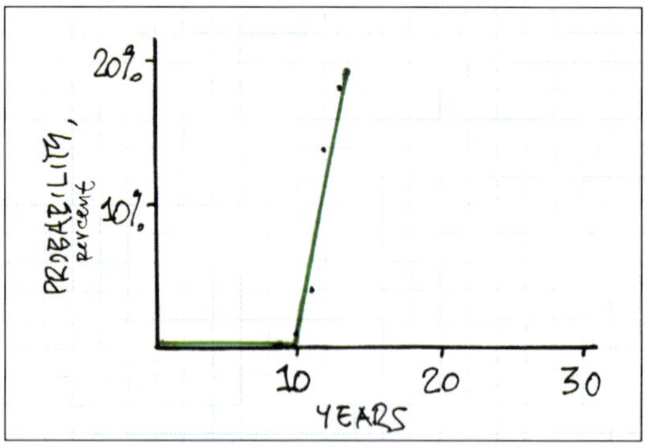

FIRECalc brand and its default assumptions

The pictures of these two sticks tell us that when we are older, we most likely can play our game with a shorter, more fun stick (more spending per year). For once, it's better to be older. Unfortunately, we may have less energy or physical ability to enjoy more spending then. We need to take every opportunity NOW to see if we can safely play with a relatively short, more fun stick.

■ ■ ■

We can arrange information we get from the sticks to simplify our choice of a Safe Spending Rate (SSR%) for our game. The most obvious way to look at the sticks is to display them by years of not depleting (shaft length) versus spending rate as shown in Graph 2-7. I arranged the x-axis to go from more years to fewer years: the older you are, the shorter your remaining game, and the greater SSR%. Once you correctly pick the number of years you want for zero chance of depleting, you basically know your Safe Spending Rate (SSR%). We'll nail down that conclusion in Chapter 4.

GRAPH 2-7
ZERO-DEPLETE YEARS VS. SPENDING RATE

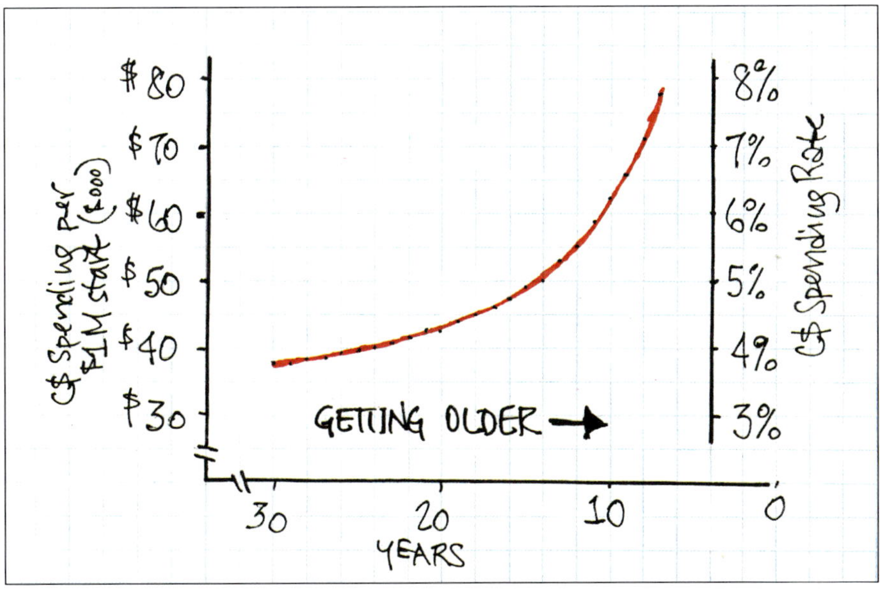

FIRECalc brand of hockey sticks using 85% mix of stocks.

Spending is constant dollars per $1 million Investment Portfolio (95% of the total). Valid only at Investing Cost ≤ 0.18%.

You can consider this a "universal graph" to get to your Safe Spending Rate (SSR%) — as we conclude in a few chapters from now. That's because the SSR% you obtain from this graph does not vary significantly over a wide range of mixes of stocks relative to bonds – over the range of 60% stocks to 85% stocks, for example. That is to say, the SSR% you obtain from this graph and its data Table in Appendix D is never too great over that range and doesn't significantly increase at lower mixes of stocks. This graph comes with a caveat: you must commit to

Investing Cost ≤ 0.18%. You can't use this graph or its data table if you don't.

[For technical disclosure, I built this curve at an 85% mix of stocks and 0.18% Investing Cost. The curve would shift a lot to the right had I used a greater Investing Cost. That means your choice of years would result in a significantly lower SSR%. I discuss this more in Chapter 6. Since it's so easy to be below 0.18%, let's just reinforce the statement: you cannot use the graph if you have Investing Cost greater than 0.18%.

The curve would wiggle a tiny bit to the left with a lower mix of stocks. That means a mix of stocks less than 85% would result in a slight increase in your SSR%. I discuss this and the tradeoff in terms of future expected portfolio value in Chapter 8. It's not worth drawing different curves for each mix, since the wiggles are small. Just use this one, universal curve if your mix of stocks is between 60% and 85%, and your SSR% never will be overstated.]

This graph makes intuitive sense to me. The "Four Percent Rule" does not consider your age, which makes no sense to me. And the "Four Percent Rule" does not mention the critical importance of low Investing Cost.

SUMMARY

Retirement Withdrawal Calculators build a wide range of sequences of annual stock and bond returns we may face in the future. An RWC tests how a portfolio fares year-by-year for a spending amount. For each year, the RWC counts those sequences with a balance that allows a full withdrawal for spending and those that don't. For each year, we obtain the percent that don't.

We can plot the year-by-year results. The probability of depleting curve has a similar shape for all spending amounts. The curves look like hockey sticks: many years of zero probability of depleting a portfolio (the shaft of the stick) and then a rising probability of depleting thereafter (the blade angle of the stick). Sticks with long shafts (more years of zero probability) mean less spending.

We can graph the years of zero probability of depleting a portfolio versus spending rate. Once we pick the number of years we want for zero probability of depleting our portfolio, we have our first approximation of our Safe Spending Rate (SSR%).

Your Probability of Living Curve

IN THIS CHAPTER...

- ✶ Your Safe Spending Rate is related to the length of your game.
- ✶ We describe probable Game Length by using a Probability of Living Calculator
- ✶ Probability of Living Curve ▸▸ Looks like a Playground Slide.
- ✶ If you are planning for just you, "You Alive" is the important probability. If you are planning for two, "At Least One Alive" is most important.
- ✶ For a couple, the probability of "Both Alive" is fewer years than we'd like to think about.

How do you decide how many years to pick for zero chance of depleting a portfolio at the start of your retirement plan (and during retirement, as we discuss later)?

A Probability of Living Calculator gives us the probability of living a number of years in the future. Difficult as it may be to contemplate your own demise, we need to understand these probabilities to make key decisions for our plan. When we plot the data for probability of living, we get a curve that looks like a playground slide: a runway, a downward slope and a flat exit. (We have to get used to the idea — we'll be exiting!)

In Chapter 2, we found that the graph of each spending rate looks like a hockey stick. You therefore are trying to fit the right hockey stick "just so" under your playground slide as shown in Graph 3-1.

GRAPH 3-1
TWO PROBABILITY CURVES HAVE TO FIT "JUST SO." ONE DECREASES WITH YEARS & THE OTHER INCREASES WITH YEARS.

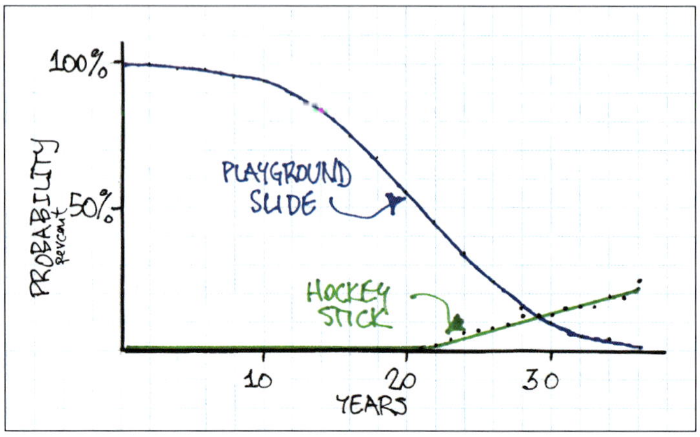

■ ■ ■

Vanguard's Probability of Living Calculator is the best one I could find. It clearly displays the probability of living a selected number of future years for "Person 1," "Person 2," and "Either." (I refer to "Either" as "At Least One Alive.") In Graph 3-2, you'll see a screenshot of the display of a result from the Vanguard Website, **https://personal.vanguard.com/us/insights/retirement/plan-for-a-long-retirement-tool.**

GRAPH 3-2
PROBABILITY OF LIVING A SELECTED NUMBER OF YEARS

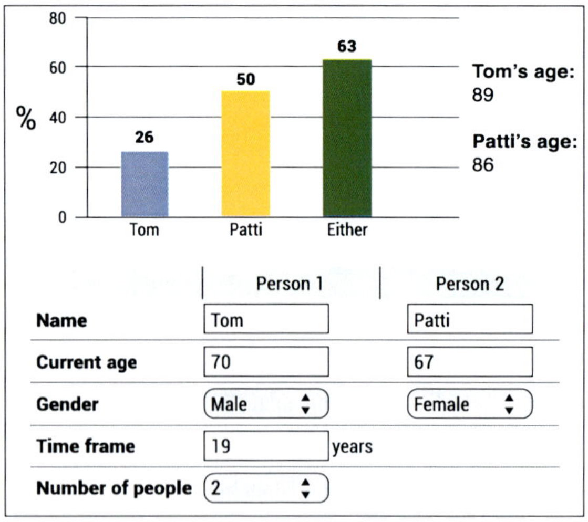

© The Vanguard Group, Inc., used with permission.

The screenshot, Graph 3-2, shows a result for Patti and me based on our ages at the start of our plan in December 2014. I increased the number of years (Time frame) to find the result when 50% of women Patti's age would be alive (gold bar). That's 19 years, and that was Patti's life expectancy. (My life expectancy then was 14 years.) You also can see in 19 years (2033) it was 26% probable that I'd be alive (blue bar), and it was 63% probable that At Least One of Us would be Alive (green bar).

■ ■ ■

Use the Vanguard Calculator to, at the very least, obtain a display similar to the one I show for Patti and me. If you're planning for just you, the important probability for planning is "Person 1" or "You Alive." That's the blue bar in the display. If you're planning as a couple, an important probability is "At Least One Alive." That's the green bar in the display.

■ ■ ■

From just the probabilities of "Person 1" and "Person 2," we can calculate six probabilities of living and dying. "At Least One Alive" (green bar) is one of the six. I found it helpful to calculate all six probabilities for each of the next 35 years. Appendix E shows our table. You can download a spreadsheet you can use to create your table at **www.nesteggcare.com.**

I decided to plot our "At Least One Alive" and our "Both Alive" curves. You can see in Graph 3-3 that our "Both Alive" curve is very different from our "At Least One Alive" curve.

GRAPH 3-3

TWO PROBABILITY OF LIVING CURVES FOR PATTI & TOM

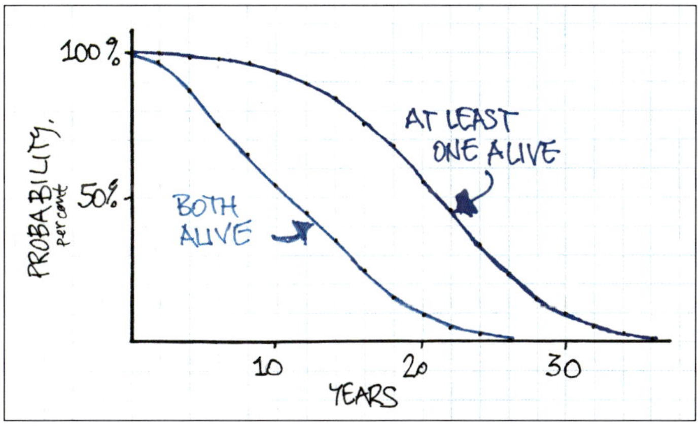

Patti and Tom, December 2014. Source: Vanguard Calculator.

As we age, the probability of living a specific number of years decreases. That's pretty obvious. That means the shape of all our probability of living curves is always shifting to the left: the runway is shorter; the downward slope is steeper; the exit is not as distant in the future. The fact that our curves shift to the left again tells us a shorter shaft length (more spending) may make more sense in the future.

■ ■ ■

We selected Patti's life expectancy (19 years) as our choice of years that we wanted for zero probability of depleting our portfolio; this was 4.40% SSR%. You can see this in Graph 3-4. Nineteen is the most years to reach Life Expectancy for either of us. Ideally, the probabilities for the years thereafter, which we'll examine in the next chapter, will turn out to be acceptable. (They do.)

Graph 3-4

Our Choice of 19 Years Led Us to 4.40% SSR%

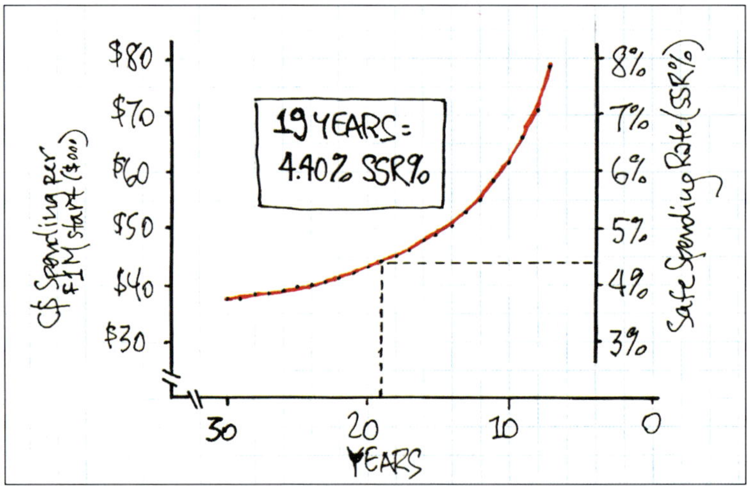

Why did we settle on 19 years? Patti and I got a clear message from the plot of "Both Alive" and the data in the "Both Alive" column in Appendix E. We just don't have that many years when both of us will be alive. From our start in December 2014, only 50% of couples our ages are both alive after 11 years, that is, in 2025. And Patti points out that the probability of these being 11 healthy, active years for both of us is lower. I put Graph 3-3, Appendix E, and the data shown in the table on the next page on our kitchen counter. We let it sit there to percolate. Every day or so one of us would say, "Eleven summers," and the other knew exactly what that was about. **ENJOY MORE NOW**.

Probabilities for Both Alive
50% probable = 11 years
25% probable = 16 years
10% probable = 20 years
5% probable = 22 years

Looking at the probabilities in the row of Patti's life expectancy in Appendix E also helped confirm that 19 years was the right choice. Yes, we can see that the probability of At Least One is alive in 19 years is 63%; alas, you get that probability from the math of 100% less the 37% probability for "Both Dead." Again, the "Both Alive" probability weighed on us. Just 13% probability of "Both Alive" in 19 years certainly did not lead us to think we should use more years for zero probability of failure.

Probabilities In 19 years
At Least One Alive = 63%; Both Dead = 37%
Tom Alive = 26%; Tom Dead = 74%
Both Alive = 13%; At Least One Dead = 87%

SUMMARY We're picking a spending amount that relates to the length of our game. We get the probabilities on the length of our game from a Probability of Living Calculator. The best calculator I find is from Vanguard because it gives the probability for Person 1 and Person 2, and it combines those for the probability of "At Least One Alive." We can obtain more probabilities of living and dying from the Person 1 and Person 2 probabilities.

Patti and I opted for Patti's 19-year life expectancy (as the Person with longer life expectancy) as our choice for the number of years of zero probability of depleting our portfolio. We don't yet know how the probabilities work for the years thereafter, but this is a good starting point.

- CHAPTER 4 -

THE PROBABILITY FOR THE YEARS "THEREAFTER"

IN THIS CHAPTER...

- The Years "Thereafter:" it's the year-by-year chance of Outliving <u>and</u> Outspending your Portfolio.
- That's a joint probability; we have to multiply two probabilities:
  - One has to be alive (a declining probability)

    AND

  - That person(s) has to fail to be able to take a full withdrawal for spending (an increasing probability).
- That joint probability will work out to about 1-in-50 chances per year.
- You can act to lower that probability during retirement.

When I think about the years "thereafter," I think about it this way: at least one of us (and hopefully both of us) has to be alive, <u>and</u> that person must be unable to take a full withdrawal for spending in a future year. The use of the word *and* in that statement means *both* events must occur. Since both events must happen, the resulting probability is called a joint probability. To get the joint probability in any year, we multiply the probability of At Least One Alive in that year (a declining probability along our playground slide) by the probability of depleting our portfolio in that year (an increasing probability along the blade of our hockey stick).

Let's use one specific year as an example. From Appendix E, the probability that At Least One of Us is Alive at the end of 2041 is 19%: Patti's age 94 and my age 97. (That also means it's 81% probable that both of us have died.) And the probability that $44,000 spending rate applied to an Investment Portfolio depletes at the end of that year is 9%. (I used the average of our two RWCs for that year for that value.) The joint probability for depletion for that year is 1.7% (19% times 9%) or about 1-in-60 chances.

I multiplied those probabilities for Patti and me for each of the years for the decade after the 19 "zero" years; Graph 4-1 shows the joint probability for our 4.40% SSR% when applied to our Investment Portfolio (see Chapter 7). For this display, I averaged the results for probability of depleting a portfolio from our two RWCs, FIRECalc and Vanguard. When I then average the results for the decade of Patti's age, 87 to 97 (my age 90 to 100), the joint probability averages 1.5% per year or roughly 1-in-65 chances in any year. Heck, let's be conservative and call that 1-in-50. Among our four parents, only Patti's mom lived longer than 87 (age 89). We both agreed that those 1-in-50 chances didn't register on either of our worry meters. We therefore settled on 4.40% as our SSR%.

GRAPH 4-1

PROBABILITY (CHANCES) OF OUTLIVING **AND**

OUTSPENDING OUR PORTFOLIO IN THE DECADE "THEREAFTER"

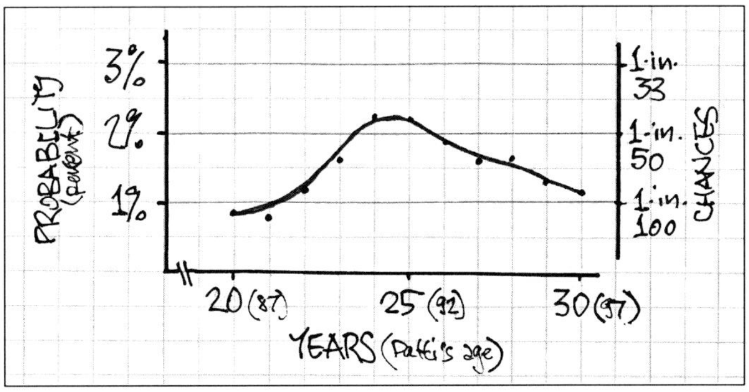

Source: FIRECalc and Vanguard calculators

■ ■ ■

For you, the probability for the years "thereafter" will also be close to 1-in-50 chances of outliving and outspending your portfolio. Choose the number of years for zero chances of depleting your portfolio based on your life expectancy or that of your spouse/partner (the longer-lived of the two). Then the probability for the years "thereafter" will be in the range of 1-in-45 to 1-in-60 chances; these are relative to my rounded 1-in-50 chances.

Your joint probability for the years "thereafter" would not exactly match ours because your probability of living curve won't exactly match the shape of ours. The year-by-year decline will be slightly steeper or slightly shallower than ours (unless you match our age differential).

If you're planning for just you (male or female), your probability of living curve after your life expectancy will always be steeper than ours. That means your joint probability will be lower than ours in all years, averaging about 1-in-60 chances of outliving and outspending your portfolio.

If you're planning for two, your "At Least One Alive Curve" will be more or less steep than ours in the years "thereafter." The steepness is based on the age differential between you and your spouse/partner. If your age differential is greater than our three years, your curve will be steeper, resulting in about 1-in-60 joint probabilities. If your age differential is less than our three years, your curve will be less steep, resulting in about 1-in-45 probabilities.

I don't think this range of probabilities is significant, so I conclude the roughly 1-in-50 chances "thereafter" should feel as worry free to you as it does for Patti and me. If that doesn't register as low on your worry meter, you could go back and pick a longer stick (less spending) than we did. This would lengthen the shaft of your hockey stick, shift the initial rise of your blade angle to the right, and lower your joint probability of outspending and outliving your portfolio in all future years.

■ ■ ■

This chapter has told us that the "universal graph" 2-7 and the data in Appendix D **are** the Safe Spending Rates (SSR%), since they meet the criteria of: 1) zero probability of depleting a portfolio for at least the number of years you select, and 2) about 1-in-50 (conservatively rounded) chances of outliving and outspending your portfolio (assuming you've picked the years in the same way Patti and I did).

■ ■ ■

Three facts add to our confidence that $44,000 is the right spending amount for us, and these same facts should give you added confidence that the SSR% you picked from Graph 2-7 is right for you.

The first fact is that we'll know perhaps 15 to 20 years in advance if we're riding along a poor sequence of returns. FIRECalc's display of sequences that depleted in the future (shown in Graph 2-4) indicated a clear pattern: those sequences that depleted in about two decades started out very badly and never recovered. We'll have a very good idea in the first three to five years of retirement; this period is critical. If returns in those years turn out to be horrible, we won't be happy campers, but we have many years to adjust.

The second fact is that we can lower the chances of depleting our portfolio by spending *just a little bit less* during retirement. The probability curves for a spending amount are for the *average* spending over your whole retirement. (We discover this if we use FIRECalc's manual spending model; we can see the effect of many variations of spending for the same average spending amount.) We can spend more in one or several years if we lower spending later to offset the extra outlays.

If we reduce future spending to average less over the whole game, we get the same effect as if we had started the game with that longer, safer stick. For example, if Patti and I average $2,000 less in spending per year over our complete retirement period, it pushes the "thereafter" probabilities to less than 1-in-100 chances. While $2,000 is about 5% less spending from our portfolio, that isn't a 5% reduction in total spending. It's less, since we'd always spend our Social Security and any other retirement income.

Patti and I concluded we likely will spend less in the future, and we decided it would not be difficult for us to spend even less if we thought we really needed to. It's fairly typical that retirees spend less as they age — without regard to financial performance. Patti and I think we'll naturally spend less for the years after I'm 80; for one thing, we likely will travel less. If just one of us is alive, we think the survivor will spend less. So if we naturally spend less, it's as if we used a longer stick for our whole game, and our "thereafter" chances are better than 1-in-50.

More importantly, if we find we are riding a bad sequence of returns, we know we can spend less and still be happy.

The third fact, which I've mentioned before, is that we're applying our SSA% *only* to our financial assets. As indicated in Chapter 1, non-financial assets (primarily our home equity) are a deep, deep reserve that we could tap for cash in the future. In a decade from now, that reserve will only be bigger.

■ ■ ■

You should now pick the number of years to find your Safe Spending Rate (SSR%) from the Table in Appendix D. Enter both the years and your SSR% on your Worksheet. The number of years you pick is your life expectancy or, if you're planning for two, the life expectancy of the longer lived. (If you think you have reasons to use more or fewer years, that's fine.)

SUMMARY You can pick the number of years for which you want no chance of depleting your portfolio. You should pick your life expectancy or, if you're planning for two, the longer life expectancy of the two of you. Generally, that will take you to a year when you're in your late 80s.

The probability in any year "thereafter" is the joint probability of "You Alive" (or "At Least One Alive") and failing to be able to take a full withdrawal for spending. When you're in your late 80s and 90s, the year-by-year chances of outliving and outspending your portfolio are in the range of 1-in-50. You can improve those chances during retirement, if desired or needed, by spending just a little less.

- CHAPTER 5 -

How Do You Use Your Safe Spending Rate?

IN THIS CHAPTER...

- ✶ Apply your SSR% to your portfolio to find your annual Safe Spending Amount

OR

- ✶ Use the inverse to find how much portfolio you need for a desired level of spending.

I applied our SSR% of 4.40% to our Investment Portfolio to get the total Safe Spending Amount (SSA) for the next year — and perhaps all future years. I used our Multiplier for this calculation. (We use that Multiplier from the Worksheet for a number of other calculations, now and in future years.) For example, if we have $1.2 million starting Investment Portfolio, our Multiplier is 1.2. The calculation would result in constant-dollar $52,800 as our total SSA.

You have $1.2M Investment Portfolio (95% of total)
$1.2 M/$1 M = Your Multiplier = 1.2
C$44,000/$1 Million * 1.2 = Your SSA = C$52,800

■ ■ ■

Complete the calculation and enter your first-year Safe Spending Amount (SSA) on your Worksheet. Let's consider this as a tentative amount; you will see at the end of Part 2 that Patti and I started with a 10% Reserve, which lowered our Multplier.

■ ■ ■

Alternatively, we can use the inverse of our 4.40% SSA% (22.7) to find how much Investment Portfolio we need at the start of our plan for a desired constant-dollar spending amount. If we want to spend $100,000 constant dollars per year from our portfolio, as an example, Patti and I would need 22.7 * $100,000 or $2.27 million Investment Portfolio. (To get the total we would need, I'd divide by 95% to arrive at a total of ~$2.4 million: ~$120,000 off-the-top Reserve and the $2.27 million Investment Portfolio.)

You want to spend C$100,000 per year:
1/4.40% = 22.7 * C$100,000 =
Investment Portfolio needed = $2.27 million

■ ■ ■

After completing these calculations, you'll be in one of three situations at the start of your plan. (I'll assume you're planning for a couple and that you want to spend a constant-dollar $100,000 from your Investment Portfolio.) One of these hypothetical couples will be you.

1. The Disappointed Duo

The Disappointeds don't have $2.4 million. They aren't able to safely spend $100,000 from their Investment Portfolio. Their options are limited: they can decide to spend less, or they can work to increase other income. They *really* need to **Obey** the rules I discuss in Part 2.

It would be foolish to spend more than their SSR% from their Investment Portfolio, since that would sharply increase their risk of depleting their portfolio in the future. They definitely should not invest in highly speculative securities as an attempt to beat market returns; that's really a dangerous tactic.

2. The On-target Twosome

This twosome has $2.4 million, the right amount for what they want to spend. They start their plan on target, with little worry or anxiety about the future. They still have to **Obey** the rules in Part 2, though.

3. The Happy Campers

Our delighted couple has more than $2.4 million. They're happy campers — and they can be happier still because they can spend more now and gift more now to those they care about. I'll discuss this more in Chapter 10.

■ ■ ■

All three couples very likely will have good news in the future. We'll find out in Part 3 that the situations for all three most probably will improve fairly dramatically in the future. They'll shift to a better situation for two reasons: 1) It's almost certain that they won't be riding along one of those horrible sequences of returns that drove their initial SSR% to a low level, and 2) The applicable SSR% increases as their age increases; the inverse multiplier decreases. They need less portfolio value to support a given level of spending.

■ ■ ■

Let's recap (and diverge a bit). Patti and I set our task as finding our Safe Spending Rate (SSR%.) That was 4.40% and C$44,000 per starting $1 million Investment Porfolio. We used that with our Multiplier to tell us what we could safely spend in any future year, our annual Safe Spending Amount (SSA).

We did not start from the basis of what we had been spending or a budget of what wanted to spend or might need to spend in the future to then calculate how much portfolio we needed. But one "might need to" expense we thought about is the cost of long-term care if one (or both) of us is dealt a very bad hand of an expensive, chronic health problem.

Here's how we thought about long-term care. We both were (and are) in good health. None of our parents had health conditions that might imply we might have super-expensive, long term care needs. We also know that it is probable that our annual Safe Spending Amount will be greater – maybe much greater – in future years, as discussed in Part 3. That greater SSA could cover a significant portion of unforeseen long-term care costs. And we have the deep, deep non-financial reserve we could tap. Finally, understanding the provisions and evaluating the cost-benefit of long-term care insurance is a complex task. We decided we might look harder at long-term care insurance down the road, but not right now.

SUMMARY Use your SSR% to: 1) find your total Safe Spending Amount for your Investment Portfolio (95% of your total financial portfolio; that's apart from a 5% Off-the-Top Reserve), or 2) use the inverse as a multiplier to find the Investment Portfolio and total you need for a desired level of spending.

When you've completed the calculation, you'll either be: 1) Disappointed because you don't have enough for your desired spending; 2) Pleased because you have enough, or 3) More-than-happy because you have more than enough. The good news is that it's almost certain that your situation will be better in the future: you'll have a portfolio value that will support a greater Safe Spending Amount.

THE PATTI & TOM FILE

When we started our planning exercise, I was retired and Patti was getting close. I was 70, three years older than Patti. Our objective was to find a Safe Sending Rate (SSR%), that is, the amount of our savings we could spend each year that would keep our portfolio healthy for as many years as we might need it. Our idea was to maximize our enjoyment of retirement — in part by doing the things we like to do, in part by gifting to the people and organizations, both charitable and civic, we cherish.

We first got a handle on our financial portfolio. It was simple for us to quickly add it all up, since it was in two places only: our investment account and our bank. We had no complexities — future inflows or outflows, or illiquid investments — to factor in. What savings we have is what we have.

I was able to construct the graph of years of zero probability of depleting a portfolio vs. spending rate from the FIRECalc Retirement Withdrawal Calculator. I could figure out how this graph moved from changes in cost (it shifts) and changes in mix of stocks and bonds (it wiggles.) I don't have to make that decision on stock mix right now. (We'll get to our decision in Part 2.) I knew that the one line I drew for that graph was going to be the accurate way to get to a Safe Spending Rate (SSR%).

We used the Vanguard Probability of Living Calculator to determine the likelihood that At Least One of Us would be alive after a certain number of years. Patti and I looked hard at the data for "Both Alive." We settled on 19 years as our initial target on that graph. That's to the end of 2033; Patti would be 86, and I'd be 89. I calculated the 1-in-50 probability of outspending and outliving for the years "thereafter." That did not register on either of our worry meters. We also understand we can push the "thereafter" probabilities lower in future years. We agreed that our initial SSR% is 4.40% or $44,000 per million initial Investment Portfolio.

In 2015, as you will see in Chapter 13, we paid ourselves that $44,000 (times our multiplier): it was a monthly transfer from our investment account into our checking account. We knew the total for the year was safe to spend. Let me assure you — we did spend it. Some of it went to finance a vacation. We gave some of it to our favorite nonprofit groups. And we did it all without once worrying about whether we were spending so much we would outlive our money.

How have we fared in subsequent years? Stay tuned.

Your To-Do List

Having read Part 1, you should have completed the tasks shown in each chapter, but here's a quick checklist of what you should have on your Worksheet in Appendix A:

1. You've entered the amount for you financial portfolio.
2. You did the multiplication to get to your "Investment Portfolio." That's 95% of the total; the remaining 5% is your Reserve. We'll discuss that more in Part 2.
3. You calculated your Multiplier, which you'll use now and in future years. (Store that number in your head.)
4. You chose the number of years you want for zero probability of depleting your portfolio.
5. You found your SSR% from the table in Appendix D. You stated it as a C$ spending amount per $1 million starting Investment Portfolio, and you used your Multiplier to get your annual Safe Spending Amount (SSA).

PART 2

OBEY THE RULES
Two Are Critical

- CHAPTER 6 -
YOU MUST BE LOW COST

IN THIS CHAPTER...

- ✶ First Rule of the Game: you must achieve LOW INVESTING COST.
  - Even modest investing costs badly distort your hockey stick: the stick that you may think is safe isn't.
  - Higher Investing Cost slashes your potential future portfolio value in all years.

The stick shapes (shaft lengths and blade angles) have two key assumptions built into them that really are RULES YOU MUST OBEY. If you violate the rules, especially the first one, you would distort your stick shape, and the stick (SSR%) you think is safe is NOT SAFE. If you aren't low cost, you are essentially flying blind. You'll see in this chapter that you would need a complete re-analysis to find your Safe Spending Rate (SSR%). Luckily, it's so, so easy to be a low-cost investor.

I feel that I'm taking a lot of your time in this chapter to present information that, now that I understand it, seems pretty obvious. I'm doing this, though, because after being an active investor for more than 40 years, I still did not fully appreciate the impact of Investing Cost, especially for this new game of spend and invest. And I'm guessing that very few retirees are low-cost investors. Most are spending money that they just don't need to spend. We don't want to be in that boat.

Rule #1. You must be a low-cost investor. This is the most important rule BY FAR. Investing Cost is the net cost we incur relative to "market returns."

All RWCs assume "market returns" when they assemble sequences of returns we may face. We all incur some costs when we invest. For this discussion, I assume that we invest in mutual funds or their companion Exchange Traded Funds (ETFs) rather than a portfolio of many individual stocks. We can invest in two types of funds:

- **Broad-based Index Funds** are designed to match "market returns" before internal fund costs. Owners of these funds incur small annual ownership or holding costs; these costs are your Investing Cost.
- **Actively Managed Funds** have inherently higher internal fund costs. Fund managers work hard to pick winners from losers to outperform the market. With Actively Managed Funds, it's less clear what we retirees should assume as our Investing Cost.

We first want to understand the effect of greater Investing Cost. I'll then discuss how to properly calculate your Investing Cost for both Index Funds and Actively Managed Funds.

■ ■ ■

Surprisingly, most RWCs ignore Investing Cost when they calculate year-by-year portfolio values. The Vanguard RWC, for example, pays no heed to Investing Cost. To be fair, Vanguard implicitly assumes you invest in broad-based Vanguard Index Funds that will match market returns before ownership costs. And fund costs from Vanguard are rock bottom. FIRECalc has an explicit Investing Cost built into its calculations. Its default is 0.18%; this is easy to achieve. Most importantly, we can use FIRECalc and change Investing Cost to see the effects. It's the only calculator I find that lets us understand the importance of Investing Cost.

The mechanics: FIRECalc deducts Investing Cost from portfolio value at the same time it deducts the amount withdrawn for spending to enjoy in the upcoming year. In this sense, Investing Cost is a component of your total spending.

Let's use the example of our 4.40% SSR% and C$44,000 spending. You can see this example in the table on the next page. At the end of a future year, FIRECalc has added the market return to the portfolio value at the start of the year. It then subtracts Investing Cost of 0.18% of the year-end portfolio value and C$44,000 for our spending for the upcoming year. In a year when portfolio value is C$1 million before the calculation, FIRECalc will subtract a total of C$45,800: C$1,800 as Investing Cost and the C$44,000 withdrawal for our spending. We'd start the first of the new year with C$954,200.

Deduction from Investment Portfolio	= Investing Cost @ 0.18%	+ Spending to Enjoy
$45,800	**$1,800**	**$44,000**

Another way of looking at this: FIRECalc is deducting a total of $45,800, and we get to spend and enjoy $44,000, or 96% of the total.

■ ■ ■

If Investing Cost were 1.00%, FIRECalc would subtract a total of $54,000: $10,000 as Investing Cost in our example and the $44,000 withdrawal for our spending. We'd start the new-year with $946,000. Obviously, greater Investing Cost resulted in a lower portfolio balance.

Deduction from Investment Portfolio	= Investing Cost @ 1.00%	+ Spending to Enjoy
$54,000	**$10,000**	**$44,000**

Stated another way, FIRECalc is subtracting $54,000 total spending, and we get to spend and enjoy $44,000, or 81% of the total.

■ ■ ■

When Patti looks at those two tables, she gives them a different twist: "You're telling me that if you were no longer around, FIRECalc is saying that $45,800 is safe as total spending. I get to spend $44,000 of that to enjoy.

"But if I had to spend an extra $8,200 in Investing Cost and be at the same safe level of $45,800 total spending, I should withdraw only $35,800 ($44,000 - $8,200). I have to reduce what I get to spend by about 20% just to pay someone else this Investing Cost? DON'T SADDLE ME WITH THAT!"

■ ■ ■

I look at the effects of greater Investing Cost a bit differently than Patti's quick (and basically correct) reaction. We can use FIRECalc to explore the effects of greater Investing Cost on the year-by-year probabilities of depleting a portfolio and on expected future portfolio value. What are the effects of greater Investing

Cost?

1) **Greater Investing Cost distorts the shape of your hockey stick and raises the year-by-year probability of depleting your portfolio**. High costs wreck what you think is a Safe Spending Rate.

You can see that impact in Graph 6-1. I plot blade angles for three levels of Investing Cost. Spending rate and stocks/bonds mix are the same for each. The 0.18% Investing Cost is FIRECalc's default assumption. The 1.20% is the simple average of fund costs for all Actively Managed Funds in 2015 according to Morningstar®.[1] The 2.00% cost is that incurred by my friend, Mary, comprised of 0.90% fund costs and 1.10% investment advisor fees.

GRAPH 6-1
PROBABILITY OF DEPLETING INCREASES
WHEN INVESTING COST INCREASES.

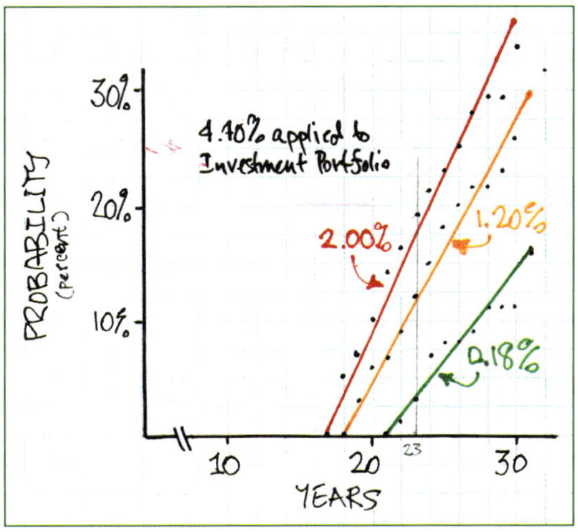

Source: FIRECalc at its default mix of stocks

What do those blade angles show? Greater Investing Cost means: 1) the shaft length is shorter and the blade angle starts its rise three to four years earlier, and 2) in all years thereafter, the probability of depleting the portfolio is significantly greater. These facts support the statement in Chapter 2 that higher cost significantly shifts the position of the "universal curve" we used to find our SSR%.

The effect on probability of depleting is striking. The table on the next page shows that in the 23rd year, for example, the probability of depleting for the two greater costs is roughly four to six times that for 0.18% cost. That means the prior 1-in-50 chances for the years "thereafter" have been sliced by factors of four to six to 1-in-12 or 1-in-8 chances. If Mary doesn't lower her internal costs, she clearly has to choose a longer stick (spend less to enjoy) to get close to the 0.18% stick shape. As Patti would say, you don't want to be saddled with that.

EFFECT OF GREATER INVESTING COST ON PROBABILITIES OF DEPLETING

	Years of Zero Probability of Depleting	Probability of Depleting in 23rd year
0.18% cost	21	3%
1.20% cost	18	12%
2.00% cost	17	19%

Greater cost leads to 4x to 6x greater prob. of depleting

■ ■ ■

2) **Higher cost at any spending rate slashes your potential future portfolio value.** I'm sure you've seen information similar to that in the table below. I show this data for 16 years; that's my friend Mary's life expectancy plus three years. High investing cost results in about $470,000 lower expected portfolio value over 16 years. I knew there would be a difference, but the magnitude of the difference shocked me. Lower Investing Cost always pays off big time.

AVERAGE OF ENDING PORTFOLIO VALUES IN 16 YEARS

Investing Cost	Portfolio Value
0.18%	$1.35 M
1.20%	$1.06 M
2.00%	$880,000

C$44,000 spending. $1 M starting portfolio.
FIRECalc at its default mix of stocks.

$470,000 more at 0.18% cost

■ ■ ■

Select your target Investing Cost. You have no reason to target anything greater than 0.18% Investing Cost. We'll see soon enough that it's easy to be less than half that cost. If you pick a cost greater than 0.18%, you'll throw all the calculations of your SSR% out of whack. Don't do that.

■ ■ ■

Do we pick Index Funds or Actively Managed Funds to result in low Investing

Cost?

Index Funds have predictable, very low Investing Cost and return about 97% of "market returns" to investors. The gross return, the return before any ownership costs, for a broad-based Index Fund is the "market return." A fund that tracks the S&P 500® index, for example, holds all 500 stocks that comprise the index in the exact proportion of the index. A fund that tracks the performance of the total US stock market holds the universe of about 3,700 stocks in the exact proportion one would use to calculate "total market return."

Therefore, it's straightforward that the Investing Cost for Index Funds is the "Expense Ratio" for the funds that you own plus any investment advisor fees that you incur. (Patti and I don't use an advisor and so incur no fees.)

What's Expense Ratio? It's the basic cost we incur to own a fund (or its companion Exchange Traded Fund or ETF). A fund incurs costs to pay manager advisor fees and administrative, advertising and other expenses. These costs are deducted from the fund and are expressed as a percentage of total assets. That ratio is the "Expense Ratio." An Expense Ratio of 1% means that each year, 1% of the fund's total assets will be used for these expenses. You could also view these costs as a reduction in the gross returns earned by the fund.
A fund that has gross returns of 6% in a year will return approximately 5% to its investors if the Expense Ratio is 1%. Expense Ratio excludes a fund's trading commissions and costs. These costs aren't similarly reported, so we can't see their magnitude. Index Funds inherently have very low trading costs, since the annual turnover in stocks they hold is minimal.

You'll find Expense Ratios for all mutual funds and ETFs at a site like **www.Morningstar.com.** The label is "Expenses" on the page for a fund. You also can check any fund's Web site and prospectus.

The table on the next page shows that Index Funds return 97% of "market returns" for stocks to investors using FIRECalc's default assumption of 0.18% Investing Cost. Real stock returns have averaged about 6.4% per year for the last 90 years, and Index Funds return 6.22% to investors.

Index Funds (at 0.18% cost) Return About 97% of Market Returns to Investors

Stocks Real Return Rate	~ 6.4%
Expense Ratio (FIRECalc default)	0.18%
Return to Investors	6.22%
Percent Returned	+97%

The gross cost of ownership of Actively Managed Funds is up to 10 times that of Index Funds; in aggregate, these funds return roughly 88% of "market returns" to investors. We'd like to think that Actively Managed Funds result in lower net Investing Cost than Index Funds because they can "beat the market" and more than overcome their inherently greater Expense Ratio. In aggregate, this is impossible.

> I'm paraphrasing here the argument presented more than 25 years ago by a Nobel Prize winner, William Sharpe.[2] He starts by dividing all investors into buy-and-hold Index Fund investors and professional "active investors." This is a good assumption: individual investors buying and selling individual stocks now comprise only about 2% of all transactions.
>
> When "the market" goes up by, say, 6% in a year, that means the total market value of all stocks increases by 6%. Index Funds that mimic the total market increase in value by 6% before their costs. The value of all Actively Managed Funds also must increase by 6% before their costs. That's simple math. The zero-sum game for Actively Managed Funds is that before all costs, their returns must match those of Index Funds.
>
> But Actively Managed Funds are **worse than a zero-sum game** for investors because of their higher costs. The return to investors for Actively Managed Funds in aggregate *must* be less than the return to investors from Index Funds, and it will be worse by precisely the difference in their costs. This is simple math: it has to be true.

The higher costs are largely the fees paid to well-remunerated investment managers who try to pick the winners from the losers. When you pay more for an Actively Managed Fund, you're hoping your highly paid manager beats other active fund managers who, in turn, are being well remunerated to beat your manager.

Study after study over the last 50 years confirms this logic: Actively Managed Funds in aggregate underperform for their investors by their higher costs.

The table that follows shows that Actively Managed Funds in aggregate return 88% of "market returns" to their investors, assuming 0.80% Expense Ratio, which is the weighted-average Expense Ratio for Actively Managed Funds in 2015. Actively Managed Funds in aggregate return 5.6% to their investors when market returns are 6.4%.

Actively Managed Funds (at 0.80% cost) Return About 88% of Market Returns to Investors

Stocks Real Return Rate	~ 6.4%
Expense Ratio	0.80%
Return to Investors	5.60%
Percent Returned	~ 88%

■ ■ ■

It's foolish to assume that we (or someone we hire) can pick the winning Actively Managed Funds that can result in a lower net cost than Index Funds over our long, long game.[3] In a typical year, about one-third of Actively Managed Funds beat other active managers badly enough to outperform their peer Index Fund: those active managers perform well enough to more than overcome their fund's cost disadvantage relative to Index Funds. That really means that two-thirds of active managers performed so disastrously that they allowed one-third to outperform.

It's not the same one-third that outperforms every year. Over a 10-year period, about 1-in-6 to 1-in-8 outperform enough to better the returns of their peer Index Fund. That stretches to fewer than 1-in-10 in 15 years. (That, of course, means 9-in-10 had miserable returns.)[4] These probabilities tell us that we'll almost certainly be in the top 10 percent of investors by sticking with Index Funds.

Those probabilities also tell us it's a really tough pull for Actively Managed Funds to get us to the top 10 percent — and it can be extremely costly when they don't. Let's assume you pick four Actively Managed Funds that you think will outperform. The probability that all four will outperform over a decade is worse than 1-in-1,000. That stretches to 1-in-10,000 for 15 years. The more funds you own, the greater the probability that, in aggregate, you will underperform *exactly* by your greater Investing Cost (Expense Ratio).

Conclusion: In our planning, we retirees must use "Expense Ratio" as Investing Cost for our Actively Managed Funds. (That's the way FIRECalc expresses it on its "Your Portfolio" page; it just took me all that work we went through to agree to use "Expense Ratio" as Investing Cost for Actively Managed Funds.)

■ ■ ■

Do you know your Investing Cost? I didn't before we started our plan. I recommend that you calculate your current costs and enter them on Your Plan Worksheet. *You* have to calculate them, since your brokerage house doesn't add up those costs — even though it would be very easy for them to do. (Gee, I wonder why they don't.) You can see how I added to get to our total Investing Cost in Appendix F. The weighted average cost of the Actively Managed Funds I owned before I switched them to Index Funds was 0.86%. Also, you can download a spreadsheet that makes it easier for you to calculate your costs at **www.nesteggcare.com.**

Very, very few retirees are low-cost investors. Investors in Index Funds hold about 30% of US stocks, but hardly any of these investors are solely or predominantly invested in Index Funds. Almost all investors — retirees in particular — incur costs that they shouldn't.

■ ■ ■

The really good news: It's VERY EASY to pick the proper funds and be an effective, low-cost investor. We'll discuss the choices in detail in Chapter 11.

think is safe and don't know it. They are lowering the expected value of their portfolio in all future years and don't know it. The only way to assure that you are low cost is to invest in Index Funds.

Off-the-Top Reserve

You already did a calculation on your Worksheet to multiply your total financial portfolio by 95% to get to your Investment Portfolio. The 5% was a Reserve. You did that because of Rule #2.

> **IN THIS CHAPTER...**
>
> ★ Second Rule of the Game: APPLY YOUR SSR% to 95% OF YOUR TOTAL PORTFOLIO.
>
> - Take 5% off the top for emergencies.
> - One emergency is to avoid selling stocks when "bad variability" strikes.

Rule #2. Tuck away 5% as an Off-the-Top Reserve. Don't include the 5% as part of your Investment Portfolio as shown in the table that follows. This Reserve is your hedge against "bad variability" of returns, especially stock returns. You'll tap the Reserve, not your Investment Portfolio, when "bad variability" strikes. Ideally, you'll sell stocks later after they've rebounded and replenish the Reserve.

Our Investment Portfolio Allocated for Spending Is 95% of the Total

	Based on $1 million total
Investment Portfolio	$950,000
Off-the-Top Reserve Not Included	$50,000
Total	$1,000,000
I apply our 4.40% SSR% to our Investment Portfolio	

Most of us probably have maintained a conservatively invested emergency reserve our whole lives. This 5% Reserve is more important when we're retired and have to withdraw from our portfolio each year for our spending. I invest our

5% Reserve — roughly one year of spending — in a mutual fund that invests solely in short-term bonds. I try not to even think that the Reserve exists. I like to think that it's under the mattress. I apply our 4.40% SSR% to our Investment Portfolio or 95% of the total. (Well, let's say that this is the plan. As you'll see later, Patti has some different thoughts.)

■ ■ ■

What's "bad variability?" Stocks have averaged about 6.4% real return per year over the last 91 years, bonds about 2.6%. Using the statistical measure of variability (standard deviation), one-year stock returns are about three times more variable than one-year bond returns. Most folks don't understand how much stock returns vary year by year: real stock returns have been below 0% for almost one-third of the last 91 years, for example.

I know I should keep my eyes far out on the horizon more than two decades away and not be affected by bad one-year returns. Our 4.40% SSR% performed successfully in the horrible sequences of returns our RWCs assembled. But looking at the details of the year-by-year returns we could face, I know how ugly bad variability can be. The worst return patterns we could face really could shake my confidence that we are safe.

> Consider the year 2000. The cumulative real, three-year stock returns for those who started to withdraw from their nest egg in 2000 was -42%; couple that with C$44,000 withdrawals per year, and the stock portion of an original $1 million nest egg could have halved in 36 months (measured in constant dollars). That's ugly.
>
> Or look at 2008. Stock returns in 2008 were the worst in 91 years, almost -39% real return. Coupled with a $44,000 withdrawal at the start of 2008, the stock portion of a total $1 million nest egg at the end of the year could have declined by 43%. That's ugly.
>
> One can look at history and find the very worst years to have started retirement. About 6% of the 91 years since 1926 were extremely poor years to have started to withdraw from one's nest egg: 1929, 1966, 1969, 1973 and 2000 were among the worst. Real, cumulative stock returns remained below zero percent for 12 to 17 years. Even though not all those starting years resulted in depleting a portfolio for decades or more, those starts and sequences would be frightening.

The Reserve is for my emotional stability, to help me overcome fear and to make sure I stick with the plan — especially in the first five years. It helps me not think about the potential bad variability of returns. You'll see in Chapter 13 that I take our withdrawal in December for all our spending in the upcoming year. In January, I have about a year before the next withdrawal. With the one-year Reserve, though, I know I can wait about two years before I have to sell stocks. I'm much less concerned about the ups and downs of the market. (I mentioned in Chapter 1 that I obtained the largest home equity line of credit my bank would give me at the start of our retirement plan; I don't plan on ever using it, but the fact that it's there adds to my sense of being able to weather very bad storms.)

My working definition for "bad variability" is a 1-in-10 year event. That works out to a real annual return for stocks of -17% or worse. We could be hit with that event next year (and even again the year after), or we could never be hit during our whole game. It's 90% probable, though, that we'll see at least one such year in the next 20. It's 80% probable that we'll see at least two. That really means that 80% of the sequences of returns assembled by our RWCs have at least two years like that in them.

If, however, we are riding a very poor sequence of returns, we may never be able to replenish the Reserve. Were Patti and I to spend our Reserve and never replenish it, we would, in effect, be spending roughly $42,000 per year for our complete game, not $44,000 per year. My calculations of the year-by-year probabilities for "thereafter" for each spending amount assume that a retiree had to use the 5% Reserve but was not able to replenish it. That assumption lowers the joint probability for depletion "thereafter" to 1-in-50.

short-term bonds. I will tap that Reserve, not our Investment Portfolio, in a year when we're hit with "bad variability" of returns. My working definition is that "bad variability" is -17% or worse real stock returns in a year; that's a 1-in-10-year probable event.

- CHAPTER 8 -
YOUR MIX OF STOCKS: A BIT MORE NOW OR A LOT MORE LATER?

IN THIS CHAPTER...

- Our choice of mix of stocks and bonds is usually driven about worry over one-year variability in our portfolio value.
- Mix actually has a small effect on our probability of depleting out in the distant future.
- But it has an outsized effect on your future portfolio value.
- The decision on mix becomes clear when we understand these tradeoffs.

Your choice of stocks/bonds mix is a personal preference. For most people, this decision is almost an intuitive one primarily driven by fear of one-year "bad variability" in their portfolio value. For its relevance to this issue, I really like Daniel Kahneman's book *Thinking, Fast and Slow*. Kahneman is a psychologist who won the Nobel Prize in Economics for his work in behavioral finance. The premise of the book is that we make sense of the world in two modes: an automatic, intuitive mode that jumps to conclusions with little evidence; a second mode that requires mental effort including concentration and computations. Our automatic mode has biases that often lead to incorrect decisions. I think that's exactly the case regarding the choice of mix of stocks. We need to use our slow-thinking mode to correctly understand reality.

You've read enough by now to know that our real point of risk and worry is determined by the hockey stick we pick: its shaft length and blade angle. To make the slow-thinking decision in regards to mix of stocks and bonds, we need to engage mental effort to understand the effect of mix on the shape of our hockey stick and on our future portfolio value.

The facts on the effects of lower or higher stocks mix makes the decision clear. We find two facts. The first is that mix actually has a small effect on our probability of depleting a portfolio at any spending rate; we can accomplish the same effect by spending just a little bit less, for example. That was a surprise to me, and I think it would be a surprise to most folks. It jangles with the intuitive, conventional choice that most retirees make.

The second fact is that mix has an outsized effect on future portfolio value in any year. A low mix of stocks sharply reduces your probable portfolio value in the future. This was not a surprise, but the magnitude of the reduction was a bit of a shock.

■ ■ ■

A beauty of FIRECalc is that we can understand the sensitivity of any of three design factors (spending rate, Investing Cost, mix of stocks) on both the probability of depleting and on future probable portfolio value. We found in Chapter 6, for example, that higher cost has a big negative impact on probability of depleting, and that you'd have to lower your spending rate significantly to make up for that effect. (Remember Patti's statement of 20% less for her to enjoy.) We also learned that higher cost slashed future potential portfolio value at any spending rate. We can similarly examine the same tradeoffs for mix versus spending rate.

Graph 8-1 shows two blade angles that are roughly equivalent in shape but have different spending rates and stocks mix. One is a $44,000 stick at 85% stock mix, the other a $45,500 stick at 60% stock mix. Investing Cost is the same. (I picked 60% stock mix since that's often recommended to retirees.) The blade angles are very similar. That means the probability of depleting a portfolio in any year is very similar. The conclusion is that for essentially the same level of risk, you gain $1,500 more Safe Spending per year with the lower mix. That's better, and if that amount is really, really important to you, go for it. (A plot of the data from the Vanguard RWC would show a similar result.)

Graph 8-1
Probability of Depleting a Portfolio: Two Curves Nearly Equivalent with Different Spending Rates & Mixes of Stocks

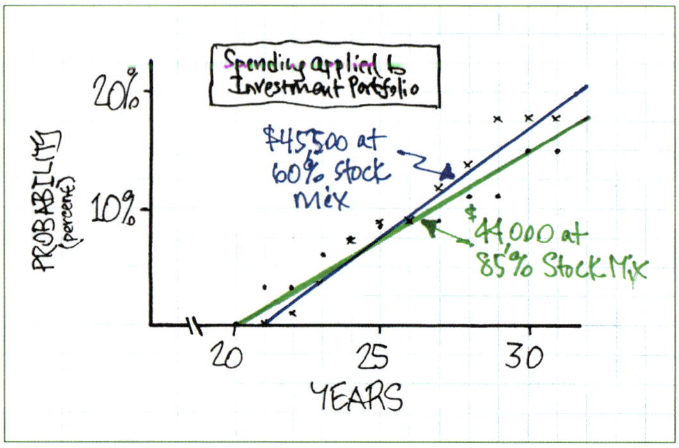

But you're giving up something for that added $1,500 per year. Your penalty is a lower expected portfolio value in all future years. The difference compounds to a shocking amount. The table below shows the difference for Patti and me would be $720,000 in the 23rd year. You could think about that as deciding to forgo a Starbucks® latte each day for the potential of $720,000 more in the future. And I'd have to use our Multplier to get the total effect.

Average of Ending Portfolio Values in the 23rd Year

	Portfolio Value
$44,000 stick and 85% stock	$1.76 M ✓
$45,500 stick and 60% stocks	$1.04 M
Difference	$720,000 More!
Source: FIRECalc	

What can you do with $720,000 more? I'd guess that's well over 30 vacations to Europe or other parts of the world for weeks at a time. That's over 50 gifts to kids and grandkids at $14,000 per gift. That's hundreds of thousands that you might want to donate to your favorite causes. Times your Multiplier.

You also can see that with 85% mix, we'd spend over $1 million ($44,000 times 23 years) and most likely would have $1.76 million at the end. We obviously could spend much more during our retirement — easily twice as much more. It's very likely that we won't have to wait that long to spend the extra cash.

You now should have the general conclusions as shown in the following table:

GOODS & BADS

	Probability of Depleting	Expected Portfolio Value
Higher Investing Cost	Lotta Bad	Lotta Bad
Lower mix of Stocks	Little Good	Lotta Bad
Higher Investing Cost and Lower Mix of Stocks	Bad	Don't Go There

That "Don't Go There" box is not a good place to be. But without running the numbers, most folks will never understand that. But we can run the numbers. Remember Alice and Mary? It turns out that they are the same age, 74, and without a life partner. Alice settled on 75% stock mix at less than .18% Investing Cost. Mary's advisor has her at 65% stock mix, and she incurs 2% Investing Cost. That lower stock mix and higher cost means Mary has about +4X greater probability of depleting in the out-years than Alice, and her expected portfolio value in 16 years is $515,000 less than for Alice. Ouch, ouch, ouch. (I used 5.00% SSR% and $1 million starting Investment Portfolio for each.)

■ ■ ■

Understanding the tradeoffs made the decision for Patti and me easy: 85% stock mix. We don't have to push, push, push to maximize our current spending rate. We're fine, in essence, in forgoing the lattes. We know to keep our investing cost at 0.18% or lower and keep our eyes and brain focused as best we can on the distant horizon. We're very comfortable in thinking that our real risk is decades in the future. We've looked at our FIRECalc results graph enough times to reinforce that. We understand that our 85% mix will create more variability in our portfolio balance, but we think we're equipped to handle the swings. We know the fire drill: tap the Reserve and if we are really worried, spend less.

(I offer a slightly different way to think about the mix of stocks in the End Notes; that discussion also supports a greater percentage of stocks.[5])

■ ■ ■

Select your mix of stocks and enter that choice on your Worksheet in Appendix A. My friend Steve, like Alice, has gone through all this and settled on a stocks mix of 75%. That's fine. If you've read this and think 60% is best for you, I guess that's okay, but I'd recommend you print out two FIRECalc results graphs: one at 60% and one at 85%. Write the average portfolio value at the endpoint years you pick on each. Attach them on your computer screen or refrigerator. Also add a Post-It® note on the dollar difference between the two. Look frequently and keep comparing the differences.

SUMMARY The choice of mix between stocks and bonds can be data driven, but most folks base the decision on intuition and emotion. The surprise fact is that mix is not nearly as important as spending rate and Investing Cost in determining your risk of depleting your portfolio. At any given spending rate, a lower mix of stocks slightly improves the probability of depleting a portfolio, but a lower mix dramatically reduces your potential portfolio value in any year.

THE PATTI & TOM FILE

I saw that almost all RWCs assume no Investing Cost. FIRECalc builds in an assumed cost and lets me explore the effect of greater Investing Cost. Boy, that exercise was an eye-opener. The rule of being a low-cost investor became paramount in terms of safety and potential future portfolio value. It was an easy decision to commit to no more than 0.18% cost (Rule #1).

It was then fairly easy for me to commit to only Index Funds in the future to achieve 0.18% Investing Cost, but this was a change: I owned quite a few Actively Managed Funds, especially in our retirement accounts. I had to admit that the fun I had trying to pick Actively Managed Funds that would outperform no longer made sense over our (We hope!) long, long game. I committed to investing solely in low-cost Index Funds. You'll see which funds I picked in Part 4.

Once I understood the effects of cost, I could use FIRECalc to understand the impact of different mixes of stocks and bonds. I saw that the benefit of improved SSR% from a lower stocks mix was offset by far in terms of lower potential future portfolio value. Pretty simple then to select a mix of 85% stocks and 15% bonds. Patti and I went over the logic of this quite a few times so we both could get comfortable. A key is that we both know what to do if "bad variability" strikes and moves the needle on our worry meter: tap the Reserve for spending and don't sell stocks right now (Rule #2), and we can always spend less — just a little bit less has a big effect.

Now we get to the 5% Reserve. That's about one year of spending for us. It sits in short-term bonds. I judge that as giving us a very conservative result: if we had to use that Reserve and never replenish it, we would drive the probability of depletion for the years thereafter to 1-in-50. I explain all that to Patti. She nods her head. And then she says, "Make it two years. Or three."

I point out that would drive down our probability of depleting to almost ridiculously low levels. And taking more Off-the-Top lowers our Multiplier and the calculation of what we can safely spend each year. I point out that there's nothing in the economy, in my view, that would suggest a possible nosedive in the stock market. "Uh-huh. Make it at least two years of spending in Reserve." As a dutiful husband, that's exactly what I do. I lower our Multiplier. We go from what I consider as conservative to ultraconservative: that extra year in Reserve means I can wait <u>three</u> years before having to sell stocks after I get our SSA into cash each December. But to be honest, the lower Safe Spending Amount is not going to alter our thinking as to "What's the next fun thing we should do?" It probably lowers the amount available for gifting at the end of the year.

My conclusion: Patti and I need to go through several years getting used to the process of recalculating (Part 3) and seeing if we have more than enough for our current spending before Patti will be comfortable lowering our Reserve.

Everything here should be shouting "Conservative!" at you. Don't add further uncertainty to already uncertain future returns. The idea is not to try to beat the market; that's simply adding uncertainty and risk and is a threat to your nest egg. Rather, your goal is to minimize your Investment Cost. Set aside that 5% Off-the-Top. (I suspect you might be exactly like Patti and take more Off-the-Top.) Pick your mix of stocks and bonds by engaging the mental effort mode of your brain. Do these things, and you'll be confident that you're on track for a successful retirement plan.

Your To-Do List

1. Determine your current Investment Cost. To do this, you'll need to understand the Expense Ratio of each fund in which you're currently invested.
2. Commit to Investing Cost no greater than 0.18% per year. You can do that easily with broad-based Index Funds described in Part 4.
3. Set aside 5% of your initial portfolio as an Off-the-Top Reserve. We first mentioned that in Chapter 1. We called the 95% balance your Investment Portfolio and used that as the basis for determining your Safe Spending Amount. You may decide to set aside more than 5%, especially if the math suggests you'd be happy with the lower Safe Spending Amount you'll calculate.
4. Choose your preferred mix of stocks and bonds.

PART 3

RECALCULATE: It Can Only Be Good News

- CHAPTER 9 -

Can You Increase Your Safe Spending Amount?

IN THIS CHAPTER...

- ✶ You must recalculate periodically.
- ✶ It's almost certain that you'll have "More Than Enough":
  - ■ You won't be riding one of the horrible series of returns;
  - ■ As you age, your applicable SSR% increases, and you need less portfolio value to support a given level of spending.

There are two reasons why you should recalculate to see if your Safe Spending Amount can increase:

1. First, you almost certainly won't be riding a horrible sequence of returns that drove your initial SSR% and SSA to a low level. Your portfolio value won't be tracking to depletion. As an example, FIRECalc shows that if Patti and I experienced an average sequence of returns, we would have C$1.25 million in 2024 and C$1.44 million in 2029 if we did not change our C$44,000 spending.

2. Second, as we age, our game, unfortunately, gets shorter. The applicable SSR% increases, and its inverse (multiplier) decreases. This means we need less portfolio balance to support a given level of spending. For example, Patti and I needed $1 million Investment Portfolio at the start of our plan for $44,000 spending. If we never changed our initial $44,000 constant-dollar spending, in 10 years, when Patti is 77 and I'm 80, we'd need about C$750,000 for that same level of spending. When Patti is 82 and I'm 85, we'd need a bit more than C$600,000.

■ ■ ■

Let's visualize what might happen in the future for our 85% stocks mix and Investing Cost of 0.18%. I show the results page from FIRECalc at the start of our plan in December 2014. I arbitrarily ran this graph for 23 years, which is Patti's life expectancy + four years. Let's assume I labeled this as our "Graph of Record-2014" and filed it away. (This is the same graph as 2-4.)

GRAPH 9-1
OUR GRAPH OF RECORD-2014

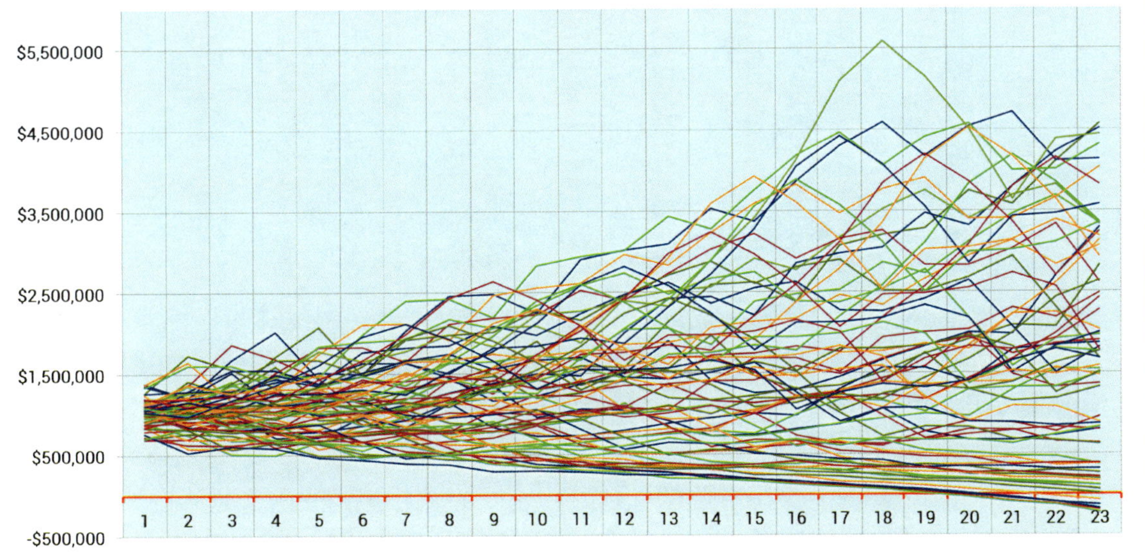

FIRECalc. Tom and Patti's "Graph of Record - Dec 2014." $44,000, 85% Stock mix; 0.18% cost. Data from 1926. This chart prepared May 2017.

Assume Patti and I absolutely trusted that we had zero probability of depleting our portfolio for nearly two decades. We **never** paid attention to annual market returns. We **never** looked at our portfolio value at the end of any year. We just kept our constant-dollar spending at $44,000 each year. (Somebody else rebalanced our portfolio after our withdrawal at the end of each year to get back to our design mix of 85% stocks.)

But at the end of 15 years — 2029 — before taking our withdrawal for spending for the upcoming year, we finally decide to look. Patti is 82, and I'm 85. FIRECalc tells us that at the 15-year mark for $44,000, the average of all sequences of returns would be $1.44 million in our original 2014 dollars. Let's assume that Patti and I rode that average sequence. I go to the file, pull out our Graph of Record-2014 and place a red dot at $1.44 million at the 15-year mark. Graph 9-2 is my best shot at getting that red dot in the right place.

GRAPH 9-2
OUR GRAPH OF RECORD-2014 WITH A DOT AT
$1.44 MILLION AT THE END OF THE 15TH YEAR

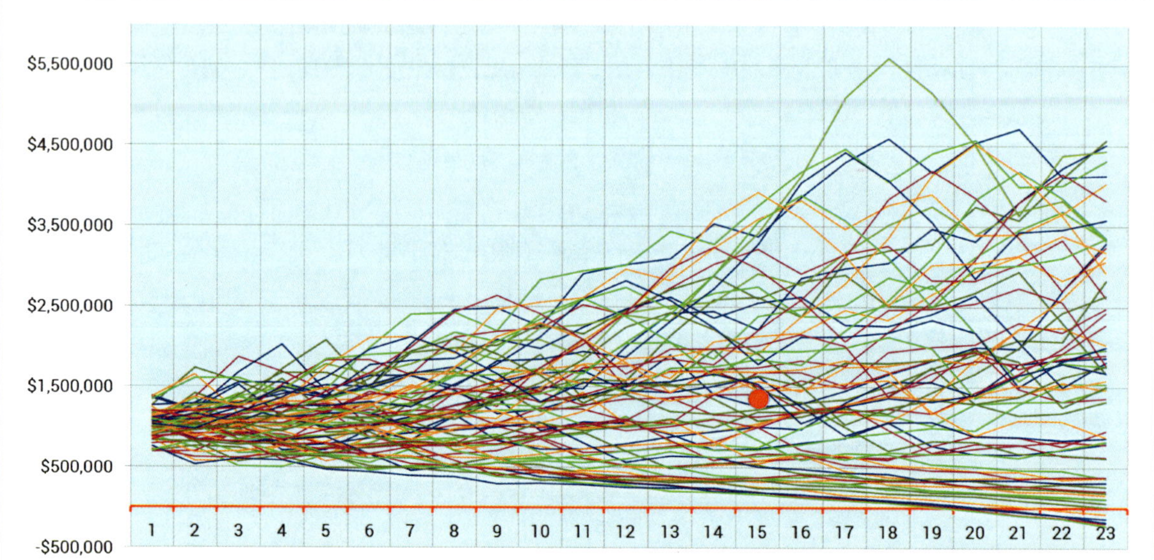

FIRECalc. Tom and Patti's "Graph of Record - Dec 2014." $44,000, 85% Stock mix; 0.18% cost. Data from 1926. This chart prepared May 2017.

I'd look at this graph, and I'd first breathe a sigh of relief that we had not been riding a horrible sequence of returns. I can see we might have had a lot less (and a lot more). But I'd look harder at that red dot and say, "Dammit. We've been living off that same constant-dollar $44,000 per year that we started with. We not only didn't deplete our portfolio, but we have lots more than we started with — $440,000 more in original spending power — and now we don't have that many more years to live.

"I can see on the graph that we successfully ran the gauntlet of initially horrible returns years ago, and it looks to me that from where we are now, **none** of those original sequences of returns bend south and decline to zero at $44,000 of spending.

"We could have spent more in the past, and clearly we can spend more now. But why the heck didn't we look at our nest egg EARLIER and figure this out? We were in better health and had more energy then. We could have done more and lived more. And now what do we do? How much more can we spend or gift now?"

■ ■ ■

What do we do? We recalculate. I'd apply the same logic and steps we used in 2014 to find our SSR% of 4.40%. I applied that 4.40% to our Investment Portfolio to get to our Safe Spending Amount (SSA), or I could have used the inverse to find out how much we needed for a specific spending amount.

Let's do that now. I use the Vanguard calculator and find when Patti is 82, her life expectancy is eight years. (I'd be 85; mine would be five years.) I use the Table in Appendix D and find the applicable SSR% is 7.10%. That SSR% gives us zero probability of failure for her life expectancy and for the years thereafter no more than 1-in-50 chances that at least one of us would outlive and outspend our portfolio in any year.

I use that 7.10% to see if our current portfolio value would support more spending than the $44,000 we have been spending all along. I multiply the 7.10% by $1.44 million. That's about C$102,000 per year, obviously WAAAAY more than what we've been spending! (I'd have to use our Multiplier to get to the grand total.) **That $102,000 is about 2.3 times what we had been spending for 15 years.** This really would bug me. Why, why, why didn't we do this calculation a lot earlier to see if we could have raised our Safe Spending Amount?

We have enough portfolio value to justify using a higher SSR% – a shorter, more fun stick than our original choice. We can discard our prior Graph of Record and use the graph for 7.10% SSR% as our new Graph of Record. Here's our new "Graph of Record-2029," Graph 9-3, to put in the official file based on $1 million starting portfolio value. I similarly show this graph for Patti's life expectancy + four years.

Graph 9-3
Our Graph of Record-2029 That Replaces Our Prior Graph of Record

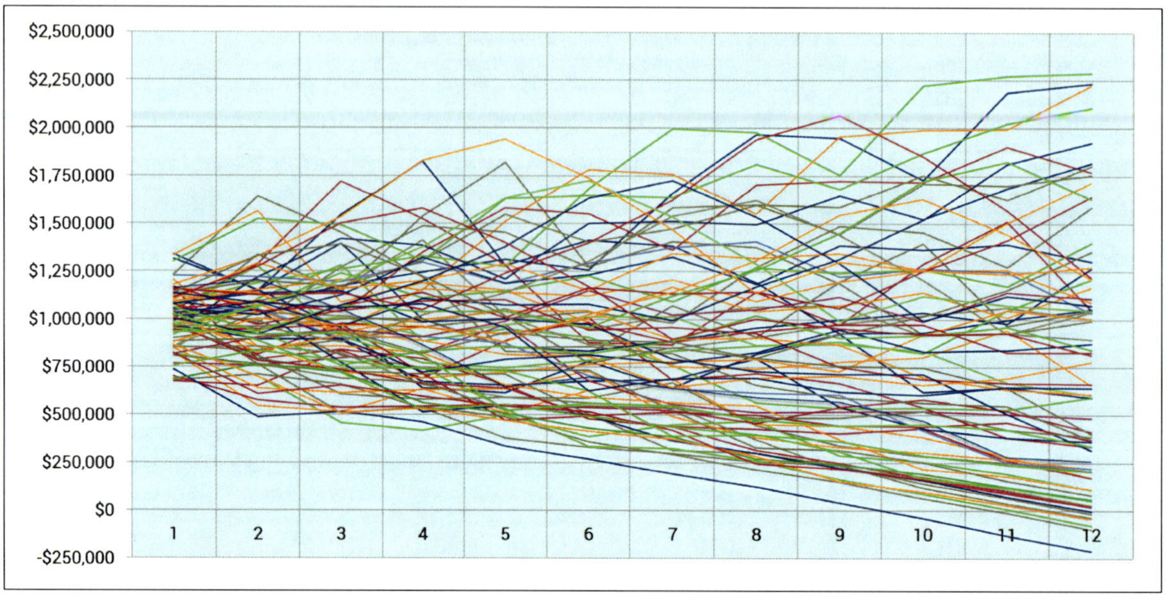

(Let's just check on the years "thereafter" by looking at that last year on this graph. I use the Vanguard calculator again and find our "At Least One Alive" probability in year 12 [Patti's age 94, my age 97] is 31%; the probability of depleting a portfolio is 4% assuming we spent our Reserve and were not able to replace it; the joint probability of outliving and outspending our portfolio is 1.2% [31% times 4%]; we're getting close to 1-in-100 chances.)

■ ■ ■

I could have used that 7.10% SSR% differently. I could have used it to see how much More-Than-Enough we had relative to a desired spending amount. We'd use the inverse of 7.10% or 14.1 as a multiplier.

Let's assume Patti and I always were content with our $44,000 constant-dollar spending, and in 2029 we planned to spend that in the future. We'd find that we would need $620,000 ($44,000 * 14.1) as our Investment Portfolio. (Oh, heck, let's throw an added $100,000 into the Reserve to make the total we need $720,000.) We have $1.44 million. We have nearly **$720,000 More-Than-Enough** per starting $1 million Investment Portfolio. (I'd have to use our Multiplier to get the grand total.) My reaction would be similar: we would have wanted to know this years earlier; while we may not have wanted to spend more, we would have had many opportunities to gift to those we care about.

■ ■ ■

The good news: we can calculate as often as each year. We don't have to wait five, 10, or 15 years to find if our SSA can increase or judge if we have More-Than-Enough. I recommend recalculating at least every three years.

I recalculate annually following the steps we've used before. I use the SSR% applicable at the end of each year to answer the question: do we have enough portfolio value now to justify spending more? Can I throw away the current Graph of Record and replace it with a new one?

The calculations we've used to date were all in constant dollars, so I need to account for inflation. Here are the steps that Patti and I follow at the end of each year:

1. Adjust our current SSA for inflation. (That means no real increase.)
2. Get the applicable SSR% based on Patti's life expectancy and multiply that by our year-end Investment Portfolio value. That value will have changed by our return rate for the year.
3. If the result from step #2 is greater than the amount in step #1, this new amount is our new SSA. I create a new Graph of Record based on the applicable SSR% and put that in our official file.
4. If the result from step #2 is the same or less than step #1, we must stick with our current SSA. I can't conclude that we're not riding a horrible sequence of returns. We would continue operating on our current Graph of Record based on the prior SSR%.

■ ■ ■

Let's look at what happened to Patti and me for our first three withdrawals for spending: December 2014, 2015 and 2016. We started in December 2014, and I've recalculated at the end of the first two years of our plan. I had some homework to set up the calculations.

First, I developed a table of the SSR% associated with Patti's life expectancy for the next 23 years, taking her to age 90. Our table in Appendix G shows that Patti's life expectancy does not decline for each added year she lives; therefore, the SSR% that we could potentially use does not change in all years. You can build a similar table: **www.nesteggcare.com** provides a spreadsheet you can download.

Second, I made a spreadsheet for the next five years to display the steps to recalculate to see if our SSA can increase by more than inflation. You'll see the detailed spreadsheet in Appendix H. Again, visit **www.nesteggcare.com** for a similar spreadsheet.

■ ■ ■

Let's walk through what happened at the start of our plan in December 2014 and the next two Decembers on this summary table. This table does not show the starting assumed $1 million Investment Portfolio and its changes over time; you can follow those changes in the more detailed table in Appendix H. All the dollar values here would be multiplied by our initial Multiplier (starting Investment Portfolio divided by $1 million).

SUMMARY TABLE FOR FIRST THREE WITHDRAWALS
FOR SPENDING FOR PATTI AND TOM PER
$1 MILLION STARTING INVESTMENT PORTFOLIO

		2015	2016	2017
	Spending Year	2015	2016	2017
	Calculation Date	Dec 15, '14	Dec 15, '15	Dec 15, '16
	Return in Year	na	-1.19%	11.27%
	SSR%	4.40%	4.50%	4.60%
	Two Calculations			
A	Current SSA, infl adjusted	-	$44,000	$44,130
B	Calculated pot'l new SSA		$42,500	$46,100
	B > A ???	-	NO	YES
	SSA	**$44,000**	**$44,000**	**$46,100**
	Real pct Δ C$44,000	-	0%	4.5%
	Excess PV for prior SSA		na	$42,700

* per $1 M starting Investment Portfolio

- ✦ In December 2014 at the start of our plan, we withdrew $44,000 for spending in the upcoming year (and used our Multiplier to get to our total SSA).
- ✦ In December 2015: inflation in the year was 0%; the inflation-adjusted

amount was obviously the same $44,000. Our portfolio return was about -1.2%. The math of applying an increased SSR% (Patti's life expectancy = 18 years) did **not** calculate to a greater SSA. I therefore withdrew $44,000 as our SSA for the upcoming year, staying with our original "Graph of Record-2014" and its 4.40% SSR%.

- (Yes, I'm sure you noticed that the "Calculated potential new SSA" for spending in 2016 was $42,500, below our $44,000. But our $44,000 was calculated assuming there were going to be down years; as down years go, I could look back on Graph 2-4 and see that a -1% decline is a very minor down. It did not register on my worry meter. You might, however, look at that $42,500 and decide to spend that rather than $44,000. You could do that, but you should recalculate more often than every three years. If you spent $42,500, it turns out that the recalculation at the end of 2016 would have resulted in your calculating a greater SSA than my $46,100 for spending in 2017. The calculation is self-adjusting. Your cumulative spending will catch up to mine, and then we both will spend the exact same amount in all future years.)
- In December 2016: Inflation was 0.3% in the year; the inflation-adjusted amount was $44,130. Our portfolio increased by about 11.3 %. The math of applying an increased SSR% (Patti's life expectancy = 17 years) to that higher portfolio balance calculated to a **greater** SSA. I could withdraw the new $46,100 SSA; I effectively have a new "Graph of Record-2016" and its 4.60% SSR%. I also used that SSR% to find that we had an excess portfolio value of $42,700 if we chose not to increase our constant-dollar spending.

As always, I would use our original Multiplier times $46,100 to get the total we could spend in 2017. And I'd use that same Multiplier times the $42,700 to find the total More-Than-Enough.

■ ■ ■

I will post each December our calculation of SSA for the upcoming year, so you can see how recalculation works for more years and how our SSA and More-Than-Enough progresses. That sheet will look like the spreadsheet in Appendix H with more years. I'll shoot to update and post the sheet by December 10th. You'll find that at **www.nesteggcare.com**.

SUMMARY We must recalculate often — I recommend no less frequently than every three years — to see if we can arrive at a new, greater Safe Spending Amount (SSA) or to see how much "More-Than-Enough" we have if we decide to continue spending our current SSA.

That calculation accounts for the potential that our portfolio value hasn't ridden a horrible sequence of returns and the fact that our Safe Spending Rate (SSR%) increases as our life expectancy decreases. (The inverse decreases: the amount of portfolio value to support a given amount of spending decreases.)

- CHAPTER 10 -

WHAT WILL YOU DO WHEN YOU HAVE MORE-THAN-ENOUGH?

IN THIS CHAPTER...

* Three Options When You Have More-Than-Enough:
  - "Pay yourself(ves)" More
  - Gift now to heirs or others you care about
  - Some combination of the above

What do we do when we calculate we can spend more next year or have an accumulated excess relative to our current spending? In our case at the end of 2016, we calculated that, in 2017, we could spend $46,100 per year; alternatively, we had accumulated $42,700 "More-Than-Enough" if we did not increase our constant-dollar spending.

We had three options that made sense: 1) pay ourselves $46,100 next year and give what we didn't spend by year's end to those we care about; 2) pay ourselves $44,130 next year (the same constant-dollar amount as the prior year) and give all of $42,700 now to those we care about, or 3) some combination of the two.

I think most folks, in essence, pick another option: they continue to spend the same amount that they "feel" is right and just let any excess accumulate year after year. To be fair, most retirees have no way to even know their SSR% and therefore when they have More-Than-Enough, so it's basically impossible for them to consider the three options I list.

But since Patti and I will know when we have More-Than-Enough and how much, we have to consider those three options. We've spent a lot of time here on probabilities, and we know we don't need to accumulate more to drive our worry-free probabilities to illogically low levels. We'd be doing just that if we let the excess sit there and keep growing.
We chose to increase our monthly "paycheck" and gift what we don't spend

during 2017 to our heirs and others we care about (Option 1). We chose to pay ourselves in monthly installments $46,100 (times our Multiplier) for 2017 spending, even though we thought we would have been just fine with $44,130. We think that by October or November, we'll have accumulated an amount in our checking account that we know we won't spend. Instead of thinking "Spend to Enjoy Now," our priority will be "To whom shall we give the excess?" We target not to save one dime of our SSA.

This choice of "paying ourselves more" also gives us more flexibility relative to Option 2. We can adjust if (when) returns dive during the year: we could decide not spend all our "pay" in the year. The amount we did not spend or gift/donate in the year would be an addition to our Reserve buffer that we could just pay back later.

Our view is that gifting now (before we're dead) makes sense for other reasons:

1. **Gifting to heirs now has tax benefits.** We can gift to an heir who is in a zero tax bracket — or, at least, a lower tax bracket than ours. Examples of zero or low tax brackets are gifts to a child's or grandchild's Roth IRA or to a grandchild's 529 College Savings Plan or UGMA/UTMA. (My friend Chet put $5,500 into his 22-year-old daughter's Roth IRA this year. Let's think of that as a present she'll open for her spending in her 65th year: she could see almost four doublings and find she can spend $80,000 [tax free] in today's spending power.[1] Smart move.) Our state, Pennsylvania, has an inheritance tax. The more Patti and I give to heirs before we die, the more they will inherit because our estate would incur less state inheritance tax.

2. **Donating to charities now has income tax benefits**, but no one gets those benefits if we simply donate after we're dead. Patti and I always will look first to make our donations a component of the IRS required distribution from our retirement accounts for other possible advantages. (I discuss this more in Chapter 13.)

3. **Getting the excess out of our estate could lower legal costs and other expenses at death.** Our estate lawyer assures us that the legal fees and other costs are unrelated to the amount of our estate, but we sure won't be around to know if that's true. Our estate lawyer is a nice guy, but I like lowering the amount in our final estate that he sees.

4. **Our heirs or charities can benefit more now than after we are dead.** Our

heirs can improve their lives and provide better lives for their children now. Waiting perhaps 20 or more years for them to benefit does not make much sense to us.

5. **We'll get pleasure by helping others now.** We won't feel much pleasure after we're dead.

■ ■ ■

What will happen to our portfolio balance when we spend + gift our SSA each year? When we calculate that we have "More-Than-Enough," we'll always withdraw our increased SSA for spending in the following year, and we won't save one dime of it. Therefore, our portfolio will never accumulate much more than our initial amount in real spending power. If (when!) we hit a patch of years of poor returns, our portfolio will decline, but we always would be on the path of zero chance of depleting for Patti's life expectancy and 1-in-50 chances for the years thereafter.

Patti and I are comfortable thinking that, by design, our portfolio will not grow and almost certainly will eventually shrink in real spending power. We're not going to "die poor," but we will die with a portfolio value that would have been healthy for our SSA for the rest of our lives.

That's the plan, but we'll just have to let this all unfold. Again, you can follow how it unfolds for us by visiting **www.nesteggcare.com** each December. I can guess that 10 years from now, assuming we haven't ridden on a horrible sequence of returns, we'll decide to withdraw less than our full SSA in a year, which would increase the Reserve and have the effect of driving those 1-in-50 chances far lower.

■ ■ ■

State your plan — at least your starting plan — on your Worksheet as to what you (and your spouse or partner) will do when you calculate that you have More-Than-Enough for your current SSA. You'll see what we wrote in Appendix B.

SUMMARY When you have "More-Than-Enough," you have three logical options: 1) pay yourself your new, higher SSA and totally spend and gift that amount in the next year; 2) don't increase your SSA but gift the calculated excess now, or 3) some combination of the two.

Patti and I decided on that first option: we always will fully "pay ourselves" our calculated SSA. At the end of the year, we'll gift what we don't spend. By this process, we know our portfolio value never will increase to any degree and may eventually decline. We're fine with that.

THE PATTI & TOM FILE

I recalculated after the first year. I first calculated our annual return rate for our portfolio. For the precise dates I chose, our mix of stocks and bonds brought a slightly negative return for the year. I looked on our Graph of Record-2014 and was actually somewhat pleased: we had dodged the bullet of a possible steep decline. However, my recalculation of our potential Safe Spending Amount did not support a greater SSA; the calculation actually showed a lower amount. I did not panic. I trusted the process and decided to "pay us" the same $44,000 SSA in 2016.

At the end of 2016, we recalculated again. Sure enough, we now had dodged a bullet for two years. In fact, we fared even better than that. The calculation told us we already were not riding a horrible sequence of returns on our Graph of Record-2014. Our calculation told us we could start a new Graph of Record-2016 and could increase our Safe Spending Amount — and that we did.

Here are some of the ways we've enjoyed our spending.

In 2015, the first year we "paid ourselves" our SSA, we knew that amount was more than we'd been spending. We took an added vacation out West. We visited friends in San Francisco and then spent about a week traveling to Zion, Bryce and the north rim of the Grand Canyon. Neither of us had been to that corner of the universe. Wow, the geology is fascinating.

In 2016, we enjoyed a walking trip in the Czech Republic. That was really a pleasant surprise. Before our start, we spent a few days in Vienna. Patti booked the hotel and did something she would not normally have done in the past: she picked a four-star hotel and room. We spent $150 more per night than Patti previously would have allowed. It was just terrific. That's where the graph of stick length versus spending rate (Graph 2-7) popped in my head as the way to quickly get to one's SSR%.

We can see that it's very likely we'll have much more to spend or gift in the future. So we started to think harder about our gifting. I'm sure we'll get better at this task as time progresses.

In 2015 and again in 2016, we helped a niece and nephew start UGMA or 529 college saving plans for their new children. We were the first to provide money for those accounts. We also added to other accounts we'd helped start in the past.

We also decided to donate more to charities that focus on relieving human suffering. In 2016 we were able to increase our donations to them. We like giving to Doctors Without Borders and two charities recommended by GiveWell that focus on lowering the disease and death rate from malaria and a waterborne parasite, schistosomiasis. (Patti has a degree in biology and knows all about that rascal.) We gave to Oxfam for the first time in 2016. Locally, our major beneficiaries are the Greater Pittsburgh Community Foodbank, United Way of Southwestern PA and Propel Schools where I serve on the board.

This tale has two morals. First, frequent recalculation — annually, if that's not too burdensome, but every three years at a minimum — is essential. It's highly probable that in three years, you'll find you can spend and gift more now because your portfolio is healthy.

The second lesson — enjoy your money NOW. Use the money your Safe Spending Amount allows to enjoy your retirement and gift to your heirs and favorite causes. There are many good reasons to do that now . . . and no good reasons to wait.

Your To-Do List

1. Recalculate after the first year of your plan, even though your real intention may be to sit tight on the same SSA (adjusted for inflation) for three years. Get comfortable with the math that will tell you your Safe Spending Amount for the following year.
2. If the news is good — and it likely will be — and you have More-Than-Enough, decide how you will spend and gift the excess money you withdraw.

PART 4

EXECUTE: Keep It Simple

- CHAPTER 11 -

PICK SPECIFIC INDEX FUNDS AND WEIGHTS

IN THIS CHAPTER...

- ✶ Go Total Market. Go Global.
- ✶ Three or Four are all you need.
- ✶ Your Investing Cost can be < 0.10%.

Both your stock and bond investments must be broadly diversified: you want "Total Market" and "Global" so that your holdings represent the broadest range of securities. That means you want to hold funds or Exchange Traded Funds (ETFs) that are total US stocks, total US bonds, total International stock, and (perhaps) total International bonds.

We have no reason to expect significant differences in return for segments of stocks over our long, long game, so there's no advantage to excluding any segments of securities. The most important thing we gain by being broad based is a smoothing effect: a broad base of securities is less variable in returns than a narrow base. International stocks have the same (or better) long-term return rate as US stocks, but the big benefit is that they often zig when US stocks zag.[1] Smaller company US stocks similarly often zig when larger US company stocks zag. The zigs and zags can offset each other, meaning our portfolio value has smaller total dips and rises. We especially like smaller dips when we're retired and withdrawing from our portfolio each year for our spending.

■ ■ ■

How many funds and which funds should you hold? You can do an excellent job with just three funds or ETFs described on the **bogleheads.org** site. The table below lists four Vanguard mutual funds and their companion ETFs. Those four own more than 30,000 securities, basically all the traded stocks and bonds in the world. Now that's diversification!

LIST:
https://www.bogleheads.org/wiki/Three-fund_portfolio
https://www.bogleheads.org/wiki/Vanguard_four_fund_portfolio

FOUR TOTAL MARKET FUNDS THAT HOLD OVER 30,000 DIFFERENT SECURITIES

	Vanguard Fund (or ETF)
Stocks	
US	VTSAX (VTI)
International	VTIAX (VXUS)
Bonds	
US	VBTLX (BND)
International	VTABX (BNDX)
Executed as ETFs or Mutual Funds held at Vanguard results ~no greater than 0.10% cost.	

The newest of these funds, VTABX (BNDX), started in June 2013. Few other fund families have a comparable offering.

Your total cost to own three or four total market funds will be no more than 0.10% per year because the cost of your largest holding, total US stocks, should be no more than 0.05%. The expense ratio for these four Vanguard funds/ETFs ranges from 0.04% (VTSAX/VTI) to 0.12% (VTABX/BNDX). You can get basically identical index funds for the first three at similar costs from Fidelity® (funds), Black Rock® (ETFs) and Charles Schwab® (ETFs) as examples. The endnotes for this chapter include a matrix of possible funds or ETFs from these four, and you can refer to the bogleheads site for updates.[2]

You should have enough information from the bogleheads site and the choices from those four firms to make your picks. But if you need assistance, your brokerage firm will help you pick; just make sure you communicate that you want Total Market index funds similar to those displayed. You always can double-check on the details of a fund at the Morningstar site — fund objectives, expense ratio and how well it tracks the performance of these funds.

We saw that high Investing Cost significantly increases the probabilities of depleting a portfolio, but lower costs don't have a corresponding effect: cost that's half FIRECalc's default 0.18% cost doesn't extend shaft length by one full year, for example. But lower cost is always good: you are ever-so-slightly extending shaft length of your hockey stick, nudging the start of the blade angle of your stick to the right and therefore slightly lowering probabilities of depleting a portfolio in all years thereafter. And lower cost increases your expected portfolio balance in the future; 0.10% Investing Cost works out to about $50,000 more in 23 years for Patti and me at the average of all the sequences of returns. Times our multiplier: not to be sneezed at.

Patti and I have our portfolio at Fidelity. We hold one Fidelity Index fund (FSTVX) and three ETFs (VXUS, IUSB, and BNDX.) Our total Investing Cost is 0.07% per year, less than 40% of FIRECalc's default assumption.

OUR CHOICES

FSTVX VXUS IUSB BNDX	< 0.07% cost

■ ■ ■

How do you weight US vs. International stocks? There seems to be fairly wide latitude on this. I think any mix of at least 20% International is fine. Here's what others say:

- ✦ Burton Malkiel in *Random Walk Down Wall Street* states that the sweet spot for International stocks — greater long-term returns and lower variability of annual returns relative to US stocks only — is about 20% International stocks. Later in the book, he recommends weights of 60% US and 40% International.[3]
- ✦ Jeremy Siegel in *Stocks for the Long Run*[4] recommends at least one-third of your stocks should be International.
- ✦ The **bogleheads.org** site shows Vanguard recommends a weight 60% US and 40% International; this was revised in 2015 from their prior recommendation of 70% US and 30% International.

Patti and I weight our stocks at 70% US and 30% International. I guess I'm dragging my feet from what many would recommend, but this is a big shift toward International in our portfolio from just two years ago. My guess is that we'll creep up to 35%, maybe more in time.

I don't find a lot of recommendations for the mix of US and International bonds. Vanguard's recommended weight is 70% US and 30% International. Patti and I are 85% US and 15% International. I've just not worked up to Vanguard's recommendation so far. Eventually, we may edge up to more International.

The multiplication of mix and weights gives our total percentage of each of the four as shown here:

MULTIPLY MIX TIMES WEIGHTS TO GET THE OVERALL PERCENTAGE

Patti and Tom	Mix	Weights	Overall
US Total Stocks	85%	70%	~ 60%
Int'l Total Stocks		30%	~ 25%
US Total Bonds	15%	85%	~ 13%
Int'l Total Bonds		15%	~ 2%
			100%

■ ■ ■

Should you overweight segments of the market for stocks? You don't want to exclude certain segments of the market, but you can find lots of recommendations to overweight segments of stocks. And here is where you can go from very simple and easy to not so easy. Things can become complex and hard to track, even though every single fund you own is low cost.

Overweighting — tilting to own more of a segment of stocks in your portfolio — is largely driven by the lure to beat the market. It's pretty much the same argument as for Actively Managed Funds: in aggregate, before costs, nothing is overweighted or underweighted. It's a zero-sum game. If I overweight a segment of stocks, others have to underweight them. I win if my overweight outperforms, but the others therefore must underperform and lose.

Here are some of the more common tilts:

1. More US stocks. Relative to the world mix of stocks, Patti and I are tilted to US stocks, and I haven't found a recommendation that is totally neutral in that regard. We own 70% US and 30% International. The neutral mix would be 53% US and 47% International, meaning that the total market capitalization of all stocks is 53% US-headquartered firms and 47% internationally headquartered firms.
2. More value stocks, e.g., higher dividend, lower price-earnings ratio. Siegel suggests this.[5] You'll find many choices for this. The Vanguard "Nine Box" on the next page shows a few. You even can find funds and ETFs that have their own twist on how they exactly define value, e.g., high dividend rates, low price-earnings ratios, low stock price relative to accounting book value per share, and others.
3. Small capitalization stocks. Siegel likes this option as well. VB is an example of an ETF you can buy to give greater weight.
4. More Emerging Market stocks, as Malkiel advises. He recommends International stocks, with 50% of the stocks from Emerging Market countries and 50% from Developed Market countries. That is very overweighted to Emerging Market countries. VWO is a low-cost ETF.
5. More Real Estate stocks, a favorite of Malkiel. His recommended mix of US stocks is 30% Real Estate, which is very overweighted to Real Estate. VNQ is a low-cost ETF for US real estate. RWO is a relatively low-cost ETF for global Real Estate.
6. ETFs of funds that employ "factor-based investing," which means they assemble their stocks to follow certain rules (e.g., assemble stocks that have had statistically lower variability in returns; trade stocks based on price momentum, or combinations of rules). This is a relatively new twist on tilting.

You can go crazy with this stuff — tilt 'til ya wilt!

But is it really worth it? Will it work for your long, long game? Siegel makes a convincing case that tilting towards small cap and value stocks boosts returns — you can beat the market just by tilting those two ways. Malkiel notes that International stocks have outperformed US stocks. These statements are true over the past 40 or 50 years, but will those trends continue in the future?

Vanguard organizes its index funds for segments of the US total stock market into a "Nine Box," and you can pick either a mutual fund or its companion ETF for each box. You can overweight a neutral, market-capitalization weighted fund by adding several of these, or you can build a portfolio with different proportions of each. Here's a picture of those funds and ETFs:

VANGUARD'S "NINE BOX" OF INDEX FUNDS (ETFS)

	Value	Blend	Growth
Large Cap	**VIVAX** (VTV)	**VLACX** (VV)	**VIGRX** (VUG)
Mid Cap	**VMVIX** (VOE)	**VIMSX** (VO)	**VMGIX** (VOT)
Small Cap	**VISVX** (VBR)	**NAESX** (VB)	**VISGX** (VBK)

If I followed Siegel's recommendations, I would expect the sweet spot in Vanguard's Nine Box to be the lower left hand corner (VISVX). But over the last decade ending in 2016, the sweet spot was the exact opposite, upper right hand corner (VIGRX). For the 10-year period, VISVX returned 7.6% per year and VIGRX 8.1% per year. That 0.5 percentage lower annual difference compounds a beginning investment to about 5% less from VISVX over a decade.

Malkiel's recommendation of heavily overweighting US stocks with 30% in Real Estate stocks (e.g., VGSLX or its ETF, VNQ) would have been a great choice in 2000; Real Estate stocks increased 40% over the next three years while total US stocks declined by 37%. Over the past decade ending in 2016, Real Estate stocks (VGSLX) have returned 5.2% per year as compared to total US stocks of 7.2%. Compounded over a decade, that difference is about 17% less from VGSLX.

Malkiel's suggestion to heavily overweight with more Emerging Market stocks (e.g., VEIEX or its ETF, VWO) returned 1.7% per year over the last decade. Stocks from Developed Markets (e.g., VDVIX or its ETF, VEA) returned 1.0% per year. Both were well below the 7.2% for US total stocks.

■ ■ ■

I find it somewhat difficult to stick with just four funds even though all logic tells me that's the right strategy. Human nature or behavior bias fights in two ways:

1. The desire for control or to affect an outcome is a powerful human tendency in all of us.[6] Spending time to search for the best Actively Managed Funds or figuring out the best way to overweight our portfolio to beat the market means more time fiddling with our portfolio. And more fiddling gives us a greater illusion of control over the future. The more important something is (and how we care for our nest egg is *really* important), the greater our desire for control.

2. We are overconfident by nature. In assessments of whether we judge ourselves as below average, average or above average for almost any task, about 70% of us judge ourselves as above average. This is the well-known "Lake Wobegon Effect."[7] Even though the chances of picking Actively Managed Funds that can beat the market over our long, long game are very poor, most of us think we're smarter than others and can beat the odds. Or, that a confident advisor we chose to pay can beat the odds.

Understanding these behaviors has helped with my urge to fiddle and invest in Actively Managed Funds. But when these impulses strike, I tell myself two things:

✦ "It's a different game now. Focus on Don't Run Out. Be low cost so that Patti and I can Spend More to Enjoy Now. Don't add another uncertainty or risk factor. Remain Worry Free, Worry Free, Worry Free."

✦ "Make it as simple as possible for Patti. Don't saddle her with complexity. Don't force her to pay high Investing Costs to sort out a portfolio that may look like a mess. Don't increase her Investing Cost and leave her with less to spend and enjoy after I'm gone."

■ ■ ■

Pick your weights of US and International securities for both stocks and bonds. Enter your weights on your Worksheet. As stated, many experts recommend at least 30% International for stocks. Few investors today hold a total International bond fund as we do.

You also should be able to pick the three or four total market funds (or ETFs) that are your base of funds — or even all the funds you'll

hold. Note your completion of this task on your Worksheet. List those funds you've chosen.

want stock and bond funds that represent the "Total Market." Many experts recommend owning at least 30% International stocks.

The simplest route to be effective and low cost is to invest in three or four broad-based index funds. If you stick with just three or four, your total Investing Cost will be less than 0.10% per year. The four types of funds or ETFs are: 1) US total stocks; 2) International total stocks; 3) US total bonds; 4) International total bonds.

You can overweight your portfolio by owning a greater portion of segments of the market, but don't be seduced by the dream of trying to beat the market. In aggregate, this is a zero-sum game: when you win, someone else has to lose (and vice versa).

- CHAPTER 12 -
THE SET-UP AT THE START OF YOUR PLAN

IN THIS CHAPTER...

* Set-up to make it as simple as possible.
  - Get your total in one place.
  - Organize accounts so you (and your spouse/ partner) clearly understand what you have.

You need to pay attention to detail and spend time to get set up at the start of your retirement plan. Once you're set up correctly, however, your annual maintenance tasks will be much simpler for you — and far simpler for your spouse/partner if you aren't around to perform those tasks.

Get your portfolio all in one place. If I didn't have it all in one place, I would not clearly understand our portfolio. Annual maintenance tasks (Chapter 13) would be a nightmare. I've had our portfolio all in one brokerage house — Fidelity — for years. If you don't have everything in one place now, consolidating is easy: your target brokerage house does all the work, but you must fill out the forms. You might be able to complete all the transfer requests on-line and not even have to mail in forms.

Make the switch to index funds. It's straightforward to get all your retirement accounts invested in index funds because you have no tax consequences when you sell funds or securities that have accumulated gains. It took just a couple of days for me to make the switch. Your transaction costs to sell securities and buy your index funds/ETFs should be less than $50.

Making the switch in your taxable accounts may not be as simple for you as it was for me. Years ago, I invested only in index funds in our taxable account, since I knew they are most tax efficient: index funds have low annual portfolio turnover, resulting in lower annual distributions of capital gains. I had only one significant Actively Managed Fund at the start of our plan.

I would not sell any shares of Actively Managed Funds and incur a taxable gain just to make the switch to index funds. You may have opportunities to avoid capital gains taxes on much of what you hold, though. For example, I've worked to allocate our donations to charities from appreciated shares of Actively Managed Funds and therefore they have dwindled over time: I donate appreciated shares to the Fidelity Charitable Gift Fund, which then sells the securities and writes the checks to the charities we pick.[8] (Vanguard, Schwab and TD Ameritrade, to cite others, have similar charitable gift funds.) You also may have opportunities to gift shares of those funds over time to heirs (e.g., grandchildren) who will incur no or very low taxes when they sell them for spending or to re-invest in Index Funds.

Grant "account authority" so both you and your spouse/partner can see the total. Without proper "account authority," neither of us would see our total portfolio when we log in to our account. I would see only my IRA and Patti would see only hers, for example. We granted each other "Full Trading Authority," which means either can trade in the other's account and move cash or securities from one account to another. If I were incapacitated, Patti would need that authority (or Power of Attorney) to execute the transactions to take my MRD from my IRA accounts.

Arrange the display of your accounts so that it's really simple to understand your portfolio. Below, you can view a portion of the account screen that is similar to the one Patti sees when she logs in to her Fidelity account. My screen looks similar when I log in, but my retirement accounts would be listed first and hers would be "Authorized." I simplified the display by taking the following steps:

DISPLAY PATTI SEES WHEN
SHE LOGS IN TO FIDELITY

All Accounts
Investment Accounts
Our SSA, Reserve + a few Stock Mut Funds
Retirement Accounts
P's Stock Index Funds (2)
P's Bond Index Funds (2)
Authorized Accounts
T's Retire Stock Index Funds (2)
T's Retire Bond Index Funds (2)

✦ First, I consolidated different types of IRAs (e.g., SEP-IRA and Rollover IRA) into one Traditional IRA. If you no longer contribute to different IRA accounts, you can consolidate, too. (We hold no Roth IRA accounts; you can't consolidate those into a Traditional IRA.)

✦ Next, I set up two accounts for the master Retirement Accounts heading for each of us. Most of our portfolio is in our Retirement Accounts, so I made that portion of our display simple for us to understand. I "nicknamed" each account with a clear, simple description (I like that Fidelity lets me use plenty of words to describe an account.) — one for stocks (FSTVX and VXUS) and one for bonds (IUSB and BNDX). I moved the appropriate securities to each account. Also, we each have the same 85% stock-15% bond mix and US-International weights after I've rebalanced our portfolio by the end of December each year.

I like looking at our portfolio this way. I clearly see our bonds, which my brain tells me are "safer." When the stock market is going down, my eyeballs focus on bonds. When the stock market is going up, I focus on the stock accounts. I like that psychological effect.

I chose not to segment our Taxable Account; we have much less there than in our retirement accounts. Our one Taxable Account holds the following:

1. Cash for spending in the year. As I mention in the next chapter, the amount is greatest at the end of December since it holds our SSA for the next year;
2. Our Off-the-Top Reserve in a separate short-term bond fund;
3. Stock mutual funds/ETFs that I've held for years. I hold no Investment Portfolio bonds in our taxable account. Years ago I decided it was most tax efficient for us to hold our "Investment Portfolio bonds" in retirement accounts.

I'm guessing your display would look similar to ours, at least for your retirement accounts. You might prefer to segment your taxable account for clarity.

Link your investment (brokerage) account to your checking account and implement the auto-pay feature. You want to be able to automatically transfer your annual SSA in monthly "paychecks," as I discussed in Chapter 10.

■ ■ ■

Mark on your Worksheet that you have completed your set-up tasks to your (and your spouse/partner's) satisfaction.

SUMMARY

Spend the time at the start of your retirement plan to get organized. If you keep it simple, you'll have less work and confusion when you complete your year-end maintenance tasks.

Get your portfolio all in one place (brokerage house). For sure, make the switch to index funds in your retirement accounts. Set up authorizations with your spouse/partner, if applicable, so you both see your total portfolio. Patti and I thought it was important for both of us to be able to fully transact in each other's accounts.

I like to organize our accounts to clearly see stocks separately from bonds, and I like to have our retirement accounts, in particular, be mirror images in terms of the mix and weights of funds/ETFs they hold. We set up the auto-pay feature to our checking account.

- CHAPTER 13 -

YEAR-END MAINTENANCE TASKS

IN THIS CHAPTER...

- ★ You'll want a checklist for year-end tasks.
  - Calculate your SSA for the next year.
  - Take MRD(s) if 70½ or older.
  - Sell taxable securities with smallest tax consequences.
  - Rebalance stocks and bonds to desired mix and weights.

If you're set up correctly and have simplified the number of funds that you own, you can complete your year-end tasks in just a couple of hours or even less after you get the hang of it. Here are the basic tasks for Patti and me in November and December. You also can see our schedule of tasks during the year on our Worksheet, Appendix B:

- ✦ Early November. Decide on donations for the year. I will always look first to make donations from our MRDs. Doing it that way never hurts tax-wise, and it could help in two cases: donating from MRD can avoid a surcharge in Medicare premiums, and donating from MRD can lead to more current-year deductions for other donations we may want to make. It hurts my head to try to figure out if either of those two benefits will ever apply to us, but I just routinely donate first from MRD in case they ever do.
- ✦ In early December. Calculate our SSA for the next year; this will be determined by the return rate on our portfolio over the 12 months ending November 30. Our SSA will either be the same (adjusted for inflation), or it may calculate to be greater (see Chapter 9).
- ✦ Take my MRD (balance due after donations) from my retirement accounts. I also need to withhold Federal taxes. (Patti's MRD starts in 2018.).

- ✦ MRD never will equal SSA, so I must decide what else to sell in our taxable account to get to the total; I shoot for sales with the lowest tax consequences.[9] I then have our total SSA in cash (money market) by the end of December.
- ✦ Adjust the automatic monthly transfer from Fidelity to our checking account; we receive a "paycheck" on the 26th of each month; I pay 2/13th in January (greater cash needs) and 1/13th in all other months.
- ✦ Rebalance our mix of stocks vs. bonds to get back to our 85% stocks mix (and weight of US and International) for the start of the next year. Rebalancing isn't a complex chore, but it will be simpler if you rebalance as you sell. You can download a spreadsheet to help with rebalancing at **www.nesteggcare.com**.

■ ■ ■

If you take your MRD at the end of the year as I do, use Nov. 30 as the year-end date for annual return rates needed for the calculation of next year's SSA. (In Chapter 9, I indicated our calculation is based on returns ending in mid-December; that's made my tracking of annual return rates a bit more complex than it needs to be. I'm switching to Nov. 30 at the end of 2017.) If you like to take your MRD in January, you should establish Dec. 31 as your year-end.

Get all of next year's spending in cash at the end of December (or January if you take your MRD then). Having a full year of spending in cash helps me avoid thinking about the monthly ups and downs of the market. When stocks declined by more than -5% in January 2016, I was able to tell myself, "You don't have to worry about this until you actually need to sell something next December. That's months away, plenty of time for the market to recover. Oh, and remember, you have a Reserve fund. You actually could wait two years (well, actually, three with our larger Reserve) before you'd have to sell stocks." (Stocks did recover for +11% for the year for our 85%-15% mix.)

I like the fact that we peel off our total SSA into monthly "paychecks." We need to pay it all out during the year, since that's the only way to keep track of our goal to spend and gift it all in the year. But that routine "monthly paycheck" also gets us focused on our two important tasks. Since we know a regular "paycheck" is coming, our focus at the start of each year is on spending: "What's the next fun thing to do?" When our checking account typically accumulates more later in the year, we're focused on giving: "Who should benefit from our increased giving this year? And how much?" This latter task has given us an added sense of meaning and joy.

■ ■ ■

Patti and I perform our maintenance tasks together. After we undertake year-end maintenance several more times, I think she'll be able to do the tasks solo if I'm unable to help.

■ ■ ■

Set the dates for your annual maintenance tasks on your Worksheet in Appendix A. I think it's simplest to establish your year-end for your return calculations as either Nov. 30 or Dec. 31. That would mean you'd take your MRD and sell other securities for your total SSA in December (as Patti and I do) or in January. You also can see our schedule of tasks in Appendix B.

SUMMARY At the end of each year, calculate to see if you can take a greater SSA, figure out how much to withdraw from your retirement accounts and determine how much you need to sell from your taxable accounts. Also, you should update your automatic pay plan from your investment accounts to your checking account. Finally, rebalance your portfolio.

These are not hard to complete, but the checklist on your Worksheet and a spreadsheet or two can make the tasks much simpler.

- CHAPTER 14 -

THE WRAP-UP

There. I think you have it. Your Worksheet (Appendix A) should be complete. It should look as complete as ours was at the start of our plan (Appendix B). If yours is finished, you have a plan that I don't think you'll ever need to change. You saw earlier that I condensed our plan to a 3 by 5 card. I keep it posted on the side of my computer screen. That primarily reminds me: "It's simple; you don't have anything to worry about or any action until November."

If I've communicated adequately, you should be able to answer questions I could not before I started our plan:

- Do we have enough? What can we spend? Or, if we know what we'd like to spend, how much do we need?
- How should we invest? In which specific mutual funds should we invest? What's the proper mix of stocks and bonds for us? What do we do when market returns dive?
- Might we have more than enough in the future? How would we know? How much more might we be able to spend or gift to those we care about while we're alive?

■ ■ ■

Here's my summary of all that you've read in *Nest Egg Care* so far.

We retirees want to answer the question: will we outlive our portfolio? We control two decisions that affect that answer: how much we spend and how we invest. We don't control two other uncertainties: our life span and the pattern of stock and bond returns we'll encounter in the future.

You can face these two uncertainties squarely if you correctly decide how to invest and how much to spend. The other way of saying this is: there are excellent tools that give you a very reasonable picture of the worst financial returns you might face in the future and therefore help you choose your Safe Spending Rate for any number of future years you pick. But those tools assume you follow certain investment rules.

Here are the steps and rules you should follow:

1. **Add up your financial resources at the starting gate for your plan.** Don't include non-financial assets. This book assumes that addition is a straightforward task and that what you have at the start of your plan is everything you have. You may find an imbalance between your financial resources and non-financial assets, particularly your home equity; if so, you'll face some decisions as to how to free up that cash. If there are other factors that might cause your financial portfolio to change, determining your Safe Spending Rate (SSR%) will require a bit more work. I offer information that helps you solve this problem in Chapter 1, which also refers you to a digital article you can download.

2. **Obtain a home equity line of credit for as much as possible.** Ours is in place through 2024 when we'll have to decide if we want another one. We all know we will face home repair expenses over our long remaining game. I have zero concerns about using that line for major repairs or improvements to our home. We'd simply be maintaining or adding to its value. Your home equity line also gives you added financial capacity and, I think, a sense of financial comfort: you've added instant liquidity for an unforeseen emergency.

3. **Designate 5% of your total financial resources as an Off-the-Top Reserve. Set that Reserve aside.** I try to think that I've stuck it under the mattress, and it's out of my mind. We invest our Reserve in a mutual fund that holds short-term bonds. The balance, 95% of your total, is the initial Investment Portfolio that is used to determine how much you spend. Divide that amount by $1 million: that's the Multiplier you'll use to determine your initial Safe Spending Amount. You'll also use that Multiplier in future years. You and your spouse/partner may decide that you want an initial Reserve larger than 5%. Once you see your SSA increase, you may be more comfortable dialing back to 5%. A greater initial Reserve has the effect of reducing future probabilities of depleting and lowering your Multiplier . . . and therefore your Safe Spending Amount. Our initial greater Reserve means I can wait three years before I have to sell stocks after I get our SSA into cash at the end of December.

4. **Pick the number of years you want for zero probability of depleting your Investment Portfolio.** I recommend that you pick your life expectancy or the life expectancy of the longer lived of the two of you if you're planning for two. "Zero" is based on data from the FIRECalc Retirement Withdrawal

Calculator; it means a given spending rate never would have depleted a portfolio based on all the possible sequences of returns since 1926.

5. **Use Graph 2-7 or the table in Appendix D to find your Safe Spending Rate (SSR%).** This spending rate always results in zero chances of depleting your portfolio for at least the number of years you pick and then results in about 1-in-50 chances of your outspending and outliving your portfolio in any year thereafter. The use of the word "and" in that statement means the 1-in-50 chances are that you are (or at least one of you is) alive and that person experiences a sequence of returns that depletes an initial portfolio to a balance that no longer allows a full withdrawal for spending in the upcoming year. Note that you can improve those chances: the biggest lever you have is to spend just a little bit less over your whole retirement.

6. **When you use Graph 2-7 or the table in Appendix D, you are implicitly choosing to invest at no greater than 0.18% Investing Cost. Make that cost an *explicit* objective.** Investing Cost is the weighted cost of the expense ratio of all the mutual funds you own plus advisory fees. You most predictably and simply meet that cost limit by investing in broad-based index mutual funds or their companion Exchange Traded Funds. You are *not* predictably low cost when you invest in Actively Managed Funds, and you cannot assume you can pick those few funds that will outperform and result in lower net cost than index funds. If you choose to invest in Actively Managed Funds, you are adding uncertainty and cannot assume the SSR% that you just picked is valid. It isn't.

7. **Use your SSR% to find the total that you can spend in the upcoming year (and perhaps all future years): your Safe Spending Amount.** It's a constant-dollar amount that increases by *at least* the rate of inflation for each year in the future. You express the SSR% in terms of dollars per initial Investment Portfolio (e.g., 4.40% SSR% is $44,000 per initial $1 million Investment Portfolio) and multiply that by your Multiplier. You also can use the inverse of your SSR% to find the amount of Investment Portfolio you need for a desired constant-dollar spending rate.

8. **Pick your mix of stocks and bonds.** Since you have committed to low cost, the SSR% you picked from Graph 2-7 or the table in Appendix D is valid over a wide range of mixes: from 85% mix of stocks to 60% mix of stocks, for example. The probability of depleting your portfolio doesn't decrease significantly with a lower mix, but you dramatically reduce future portfolio values with a lower mix. Your real risk of depleting your portfolio is years in the future — perhaps decades. But if you would be an emotional

basket case when stocks decline — and it's 90% probable that we'll see at least one year of -17% return for stocks in the next 20 years and 80% probable that we'll see at least two — you'll be more comfortable with a lower mix of stocks.

9. **Select your weights for US and International securities.** We have no reason to expect that either US or International securities will outperform the other in the future. But you want both US and International securities because of the smoothing effect on your portfolio: one often zigs while the other zags. This smoothing effect is most important now that you're withdrawing annually from your portfolio for spending.

10. **Pick specific broad-based mutual funds or their companion Exchange Traded Funds.** Your total weighted investment cost for Index Funds likely will be less than 0.10% because your largest holding, US stocks, will have a cost no greater than 0.05%. Choose broad-based funds: total US stocks, etc., not just segments of the market. You can pick just three or four funds and wind up owning pieces of over 30,000 securities, roughly all the securities traded in the world. You could decide to overweight segments of stocks, such as smaller capitalization stocks or value (e.g., higher-dividend) stocks. Overweighting is largely driven by the lure of beating the market and is a zero-sum game. Your overweighting may win in the long run, but someone else has to decide to underweight and then wind up losing. You can get overly complex with weighting in my opinion. I try to keep it simple by asking, "What would Patti do with this portfolio if I no longer were around?"

11. **Recalculate your Safe Spending Amount — the amount you pay yourself each year — frequently.** I recommend you recalculate at least every three years; I recalculate annually. Your SSA may remain the same (But always adjust for inflation.) or it may increase by more than inflation. That's because: 1) it's almost certain you won't be riding one of those horrible sequences of returns that drove your initial SSA to a low level, and 2) your applicable SSR% increases as you age; you need less portfolio value to support a given amount of spending. *Nest Egg Care* points you to two spreadsheet templates that are of help.

12. **Set up your plan so that you and your life partner, if applicable, both clearly understand it when you each log in to the brokerage where you keep your financial resources.** We keep ours all in one place (Fidelity). I have combined different kinds of IRA accounts into one for each of us. I prefer two accounts that separate our two stock funds from our two bond

funds. I like that we can "nickname" the accounts so we easily understand what's in them.

13. **List your year-end maintenance tasks.** Take a look at our checklist and timing as an example (Appendix B). The key tasks are: calculate your return rate for the year to determine if your SSA can increase by more than inflation; sell securities in your IRA account for your MRD (if over 70½) and also in your taxable account to get to your total SSA for the upcoming year; rebalance your accounts back to your designed mix of stocks and bonds; determine how you will "pay yourself" the SSA you have calculated. We pay ourselves 2/13 in January and 1/13 in all other months.

THE PATTI & TOM FILE

When Patti and I prepared for our year-end maintenance tasks at the end of our first CORE year, we shared a sense of anxiety. We knew it had been a down year for stocks generally, and I think we both wondered if we would have the determination to follow through on our plan in the face of negative returns. We did, keeping our Safe Spending Rate, and therefore our Safe Spending Amount, the same.

With two years of experience — and a Safe Spending Amount that we've been able to raise — our attitude has changed. We're better at the mechanics of the exercise, but more importantly, we approach year-end maintenance with a sense of excitement. Will we be able to increase our spending again? What shall we do with the extra cash? Vacations? Donations?

These are delightful dilemmas. You'll enjoy plenty of them if you stick to your plan.

Your To-Do List

If you've completed all the steps listed above, you've done it all. Congratulations! Get out there and enjoy your retirement. NOW.

Endnotes

Introduction — Why I Wrote This Book

1. The "Four Percent Rule" is a rule of thumb that you can safely withdraw 4% from a starting portfolio, and the amount withdrawn can be increased annually to keep pace with inflation. You can read about the history of the Four Percent Rule at this Wikipedia entry: **https://en.wikipedia.org/wiki/William_Bengen.** Some other sites that have definitions, descriptions or discussions of this rule are at **Investopedia.com, boggleheads.org,** and **http://rootofgood.com/four-percent-rule-fixed-variable-percent-withdrawal/.** Other background information that may be of interest is at **https://en.wikipedia.org/wiki/Trinity_study** and **https://en.wikipedia.org/wiki/Retirement_spend-down**.

Part 1 – Choose Your SAFE SPENDING RATE

1. *Stocks for the Long Run,* Jeremy Siegel, Fifth Edition, 2014, McGraw-Hill, Chapter 5. The data shown is from 1926 through 2012. Returns for stocks (table on page 83) have been surprisingly steady over different, long periods of time since 1802. The book has an interesting discussion on the history of measuring annual returns for stocks and bond returns, relatively accurately, all the way back to 1802. The measures of US stock returns are most comprehensive from 1926 as assembled by the Center for Research in Security Prices.

   Siegel's graph on page 6 is the plot the compound growth of stocks and of bonds since 1802. I think I remember his graph from his first edition, and it's imprinted in my brain. One dollar invested in stocks in 1802 compounded in real spending power (no inflation) to over $700,000 today (data through 2012) while $1 invested in bonds compounded to about $1,800. Stocks grew "only" about 400 times more.

Part 2 — OBEY The Rules

1. Simple average is the same as arithmetic average — the sum of all fund expense ratios divided by the number of funds. The weighted average (weighted by funds invested) in 2015 that I mention later was 0.80%.

2. William Sharpe won the Nobel Prize in economics in 1990. A good explanation of Sharpe's 1991 article is in the book *The Great Mutual Fund Trap,* Gregory Baer and Gary Gensler, Broadway Books, 2002. Sharpe's original article was from "The Financial Analysts Journal Vol. 47," January/February 1991, pages 7-9. You can read the article here: **https://web.stanford.edu/~wfsharpe/art/active/active.htm**

3. I like the discussion in *Thinking, Fast and Slow,* Daniel Kahneman, Farrar, Strauss, and Giroux, 2011. I mention this book again in Chapter 8. We have an automatic, intuitive mode of thinking to understand reality, and we have a computational mode that we have to engage to understand reality. Our bias is to rely on our automatic mode, but it often makes incorrect decisions. To accurately understand reality we must work to engage our slow thinking mode.

   Chapter 20 in *Thinking Fast* . . . is titled, "Overconfidence and The Illusion of Skill." Our automatic mode is overconfident and biased to think we have more skill than we do, and it assumes others have more skill than they do. Stock-picking demonstrates a bias of our automatic mode: the illusion of skill and belief that others have skill. Most individual investors automatically think financial experts are smart; they know these experts are hard working. And the experts exude confidence. Therefore, investors think they're obtaining value by paying experts to beat the market. But the overwhelming evidence is that these engaging, hard workers do not beat the market.

   The financial industry "appears to be built largely on an illusion of skill." "Financial professionals are able to extract a considerable amount of wealth from amateurs [but] few stock pickers, if any, have the skill needed to beat the market consistently, year after year . . . The evidence from more than 50 years of research is . . . the selection of stocks is more like rolling dice. The year-to-year correlation of outcomes is very small, barely higher than zero."

   The financial industry cannot absorb or digest the evidence that, in aggregate, it demonstrates no skill, since the industry's belief in skill is ingrained. For financial professionals to think otherwise threatens their livelihood and self-worth.

■ ■ ■

I particularly like chapters 9 and 10 that deal with stocks and bonds and financial returns in *The Drunkard's Walk. How Randomness Rules Our Lives,*

Leonard Mlodinow, Pantheon Books, 2008. This has a similar message to Kahneman's.

We have a bias or behavioral characteristic to see patterns where no patterns exist. If we assembled 4,000 robots as mutual fund managers that randomly picked stocks, there would be some who outperform and others who underperform following an expected pattern for random results. The actual results of managers vary little from the random pattern we'd expect. It's very hard to deduce that experts have skill to outperform. Someone's results always will be much better than average, but we don't know in advance who that will be.

When we look at the past, we can arrange outcomes to make them seem very orderly. Since the past appears orderly, we think the future is orderly. We look at the past performance of mutual funds and can order performance from best to worst. When we look at that ordering, our brains assume that the ordering will be the same in the future: the best will continue to be the best. A related bias is the "hot hand fallacy." We think a string of successes for mutual fund managers, for example, must mean they have a hot hand or genuine skill when it's really the random nature of results.

The graph below is an example of the ranking of 800 mutual funds managers over five years. If the past were a good predictor of the future, we'd expect for the subsequent five-year period that the winners in the left graph would be the winners in the graph on the right. But the graph of the next five-year period of results shows that performance winds up looking like random noise.

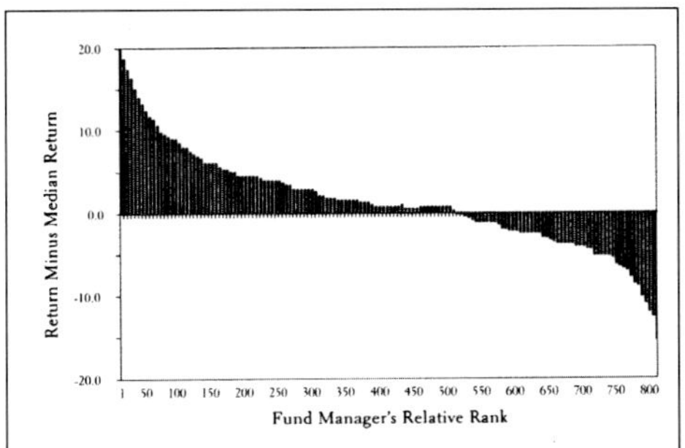

Performance versus ranking of the top mutual funds in the five-year period 1991–1995.

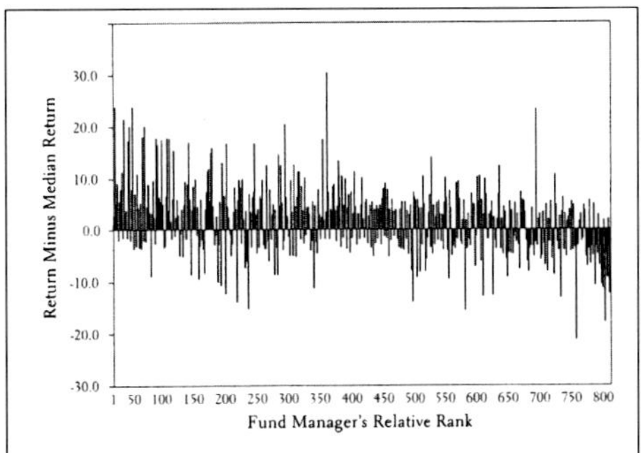

How the top funds in 1991–1995 performed in 1996–2000.

We assign skill to those who hold themselves as experts. We're trusting. The more confident and successful people appear, the more we trust them. The stocks recommended by prognosticators on the television show Wall Street

Week lagged far behind the market. A study of 153 newsletters found "no significant evidence of stock-picking ability."

4. You can download this 19-page study for more detail: "The case for index-fund investing," Vanguard, March 2015. Over a 10-year period ending December 2014, about 1-in-10 Large Blend mutual funds (largest category of funds) outperformed their benchmark index. **https://personal.vanguard.com/pdf/s296.pdf**

   You also can download the original June 2015 14-page report: "Morningstar's Active/Passive Barometer: a new yardstick for an old debate," and its most recent March 2017 update. This report measures the performance of Actively Managed Funds relative to their peer Index Fund (after Index Fund fees). Over a 10-year period ending Dec. 31, 2016, 14% of Active US Large Blend funds outperformed their benchmark Index Fund. (That's a slightly higher percentage than reported by Vanguard.) The average Active Large Blend fund underperformed its benchmark Index Fund by 1.2% per year over the trailing decade.

   http://corporate.morningstar.com/US/documents/ResearchPapers/MorningstarActive-PassiveBarometerJune2015.pdf and https://corporate1.morningstar.com/ResearchLibrary/article/796672/the-morningstar-activepassive-barometer---year-end-2016/

   The April 14, 2017 Wall Street Journal article "Indexers Best Stock Pickers Even Over 15 Years" contains a Table that shows that actively managed funds failed to beat their respective benchmark index: 92% of Large-Cap (S&P 500), 95% of Mid-Cap (S&P MidCal 400), and 93% of Small-Cap (S&P SmallCap 600) failed to outperform over 15 years. (You have to be a subscriber to read the on-line version of the article.)

   This is a fun audio on Warren Buffet's bet on index funds vs. hedge funds: **http://www.npr.org/2016/03/10/469897691/armed-with-an-index-fund-warren-buffett-is-on-track-to-win-hedge-fund-bet**

5. I like Siegel's table (*Stocks for the Long Run,* page 96) of the probability that stocks will outperform bonds over different holding periods. You can see my summary table on the next page. The expected return rates for stocks are greater than for bonds (6.4% vs. 2.6%), but because of the greater variability of stock returns, bonds have outperformed stocks a greater percentage of the time than you might think: bonds outperform stocks nearly 40% of the

time for one-year holding periods. But it's an increasing probability that stocks outperform bonds as the holding period lengthens, and the probability that stocks outperform bonds eventually approaches 100%.

Percentage of Time Stocks Outperform Bonds & Difference in Expected Value

		Expected Value $1,000		
Holding Period, Yrs.	Stocks outperform	Stocks @ 6.4%	Bonds @ 2.6%	Growth Difference
1	61%	$1,064	$1,026	$38
3	69%	$1,205	$1,080	$125
5	69%	$1,364	$1,137	$227
10	78%	$1,860	$1,293	$567
20	96%	$3,458	$1,671	$1,787
30	99%	$6,431	$2,160	$4,271

Data from 1871 to 2012

I added several columns to his table. I show the expected value of stocks and bonds for the holding periods shown, and I show the dollar difference in the expected growth of an initial $1,000. At the three-year mark, stocks outperform bonds about 70% of the time, but the expected dollar return difference between stocks and bonds is not large.

By the five-year mark when stocks outperform, the difference in expected value from compound growth starts to become significant; the expected growth of stocks ($364 per $1,000 start) is more than 2.5 times that of bonds ($137 per $1,000 start). With more years, the difference in expected value expands; you see the effect of compounding of return differences. At the 10-year mark, for example, stocks outperform bonds about 80% of the time and the $567 added expected growth from stocks is about 15 times that of the 1-year $38 growth difference. That growth difference is compounding at a very high rate — roughly 20% per year.

■ ■ ■

Siegel provides a graph on page 95 that shows the lowest and highest cumulative returns for stocks and bonds for different holding periods. I summarize the lowest returns in the table on the next page. You can see that at the five-year mark, the worst compound annual stock returns for stocks are similar to that for bonds. After that the worst compound annual return for stocks is better than the worst return for bonds.

Lowest Compound Annual Real Returns

Holding Period	Stocks	Bonds
1 year	-38.6%	-21.9%
2 years	-31.7%	-15.9%
5 years	-11.9%	-10.1%
10 years	-4.1%	-5.4%
20 years	+1.0%	-3.1%

Data from 1802-2012

Worst stock returns better than worst bond returns

The message I get from looking at these two tables is that it makes sense to own a greater and greater portion of stocks as the holding period lengthens, and for some future year it makes no sense to hold bonds.

■ ■ ■

We can view our nest egg as a stack of one-year slices that we're going to withdraw for spending each future year. We take the first slice off the top for spending in the first year. That next slice will sit there a year before we take it; it will be two years for the next one, and so on; each slice has a longer holding period. The slices we hold for the first two years should have a healthy portion of bonds, largely because a bad returns for stocks can be much worse than a bad returns for bonds. But by the fifth year, a really bad return for stocks is similar to a really bad return for bonds; that slice should hold a significant portion of stocks, because the expected return for stocks is also far outpacing bonds. Clearly the 10-year slice, in my opinion, should be all stocks: 1) the worst return rate for stock is not as bad as for bonds; 2) it's 80% probable that stocks will outperform; and 3) the expected return from stocks is almost triple that of bonds. All subsequent slices should be all stocks.

Patti and I have roughly a +20 year time horizon. When I add up my sketch of the slice-by-slice proportion of stocks vs. bonds that makes sense to me, I get to more than 80% stocks in total. The analytical steps using our two RWCs are the correct way to pick our mix of stocks vs. bonds, but this different look supports the logic of a greater percentage of stocks.

Part 3 — RECALCULATE

1. I'm using the rough "Rule of 72" for my counting of doublings: 72 divided by the annual interest rate percentage gives the approximate number years for an initial investment to double. 72/6.4% = 11.25 years for one doubling. It's 43 years to age 65 for Chet's daughter. That's about 3.8 doublings, which, for $5,500, works out to $80,000. Had I used the future-value calculation in Excel®, I would have found $5,500 compounded to $79,000. See **https://en.wikipedia.org/wiki/Rule_of_72**

Part 4 – EXECUTE

1. Folks much smarter than I use math methods to measure the degree of zig and zag for different types of securities. The math result is called "correlation coefficient." The message of the math is that it's good to combine security types that have a measure of one going up when the other is going down and vice versa (are not perfectly correlated). The result is less overall variability in returns. Fundamentally, that's why we combine stocks and bonds, large capitalization stocks and small capitalization stocks, US stocks and International stocks and so on. I liked the discussion on this topic in *A Random Walk Down Wall Street,* 11th edition, Burton Malkiel, WW Norton & Company, Chapter 8.

   As retirees, we want to invest to have less variability in the probability of depleting our portfolio, and our first chance of depleting is typically decades away. Our concern is the number of years that represent the shaft of our hockey stick and the slope of its blade angle thereafter. We learned in this book the factors that affect changes in shaft length, (primarily spending rate and investing cost, and then mix of stocks and bonds to a lesser degree) which then affect the height of the blade angle in all future years. That's a different concept of variability than the math of correlation coefficients, which focuses on variability one-year returns.

2. Choices from these four fund families result in low Investing Cost, less than 0.10% for your total portfolio:

FOUR FUND FAMILIES
FUNDS & ETF - EXCHANGE TRADED FUNDS

Fund Type	Fidelity	Vanguard	Blackrock®	Charles Schwab®
Stock				
Total US	FSTMX/FSTVX	VTSMX/VTSAX (VTI)	ITOT	SCHB
Total Int'l	FTIGX/FTIPX	VGTSX/VTIAX (VXUS)	IXUS	SCHF
Bond				
Total US	FBIDX/FSITX	VBMFX/VBTLX (BND)	AGG or IUSB	SCHZ
Total Int'l	na	VTIBX/VTABX (BNDX)	na	na
Number of Securities	9,600	31,100	12,900	6,300

See boglehead.org for updates and details
First fund listed has higher Expense Ratio but lower minimum investment

3. In *Random Walk. . .* Malkiel describes the benefit of holding International stocks in Chapter 8 starting on page 201. Over a +40-year period through 2013, International stocks have outperformed US stocks by about 0.7% per year. (That difference would have compounded to about 33% greater total return from International stocks.) But annual returns from International stocks have been about 25% more variable than for US stocks. Because of the patterns of zigs and zags (not Malkiel's term!), the paradoxical result is that a weight of about 80% US and 20% International stocks delivers two good results: relative to US stocks only, that mix boosts returns and (the paradox) lowers annual variability in returns.

   Malkiel displays a model portfolio for aging Baby Boomers on page 389. He recommends 60% US and 40% International for stocks while US should be 30% Real Estate equities. He suggests International stocks should be split evenly between Developed and Emerging Markets. His percentages for US Real Estate and for Emerging Markets very significantly overweight these two segments. He's primarily overweighting them because of their historical smoothing effect when US stocks have tanked, primarily in the horrible pattern of returns over three years starting in 2000, not because he believes they are good bets to outperform over the long run.

4. In *Stocks for the Long Run,* Siegel's "Guides to Successful Investing" starts on page 374. He recommends at least one-third of an equity portfolio be invested in International stocks, currently defined as those not headquartered in the US. "Today the United States has only about one-half of the world's equity capital, and that fraction is declining rapidly. Owning foreign stocks is a must in today's global economy."

5. Siegel in *Stocks . . .* advises tilting your portfolio to value stocks — those with lower P/E ratios and higher dividend yields – and to smaller capitalization

stocks. His discussion on the benefits of value stocks starts on page 179. His case for tilting to smaller capitalization stocks begins on page 176.

6. I enjoyed the discussion on our human bias to want to control the future in *Drunkard's Walk: How Randomness Rules Our Lives* by Leonard Mlodinow and in *Stumbling on Happiness* by Daniel Gilbert. We humans have a strong urge to try to affect an uncertain future. That urge to act also leads us to think that more complexity is better than simplicity. My friend, Mary, looks at her stock portfolio of about 30 (costly) actively managed funds and thinks that's better diversification than two broad-based index funds that own every single stock in the world.

   Random Walk. . . also offers a good discussion of why investors behave irrationally when investing. Malkiel discusses four factors: overconfidence (far too optimistic view of their skills in picking stocks or Actively Managed Mutual Funds), biased judgments (including the desire for control and the tendency to find patterns in randomness), herd mentality (everyone follows the same strategies and owns the same stocks) and loss aversion (we make irrational decisions about when to sell a stock).

7. You can read more on The Lake Wobegon Effect at **https://en.wikipedia.org/wiki/Illusory_superiority.** Check out this fun audio: **http://www.sciencefriday.com/segments/are-all-minnesotans-above-average/**. And you'll enjoy this interesting article about British prisoners (two-thirds convicted of violent crimes) and their judgments that they are more moral, trustworthy and compassionate than the general population: **http://www.economist.com/blogs/babbage/2014/03/social-psychology**

8. Fidelity has a cool tool that allows me to donate "specific shares" to the Fidelity Charitable Gift Fund (**https://www.fidelitycharitable.org**). The tool quickly arranges my holdings in a mutual fund (held at Fidelity Investments) by lowest-cost shares to highest-cost shares. It's easy to donate the lowest-cost shares for the best tax advantage. That means the shares I eventually have to sell in my Taxable account will then be higher-cost shares resulting in lower capital gains and taxes. To donate, I ask the FCGF to send checks to the charities I recommend. (FCGF sells the shares I donate to it the day they receive them.)

9. Fidelity's tool also can arrange each historical share purchase for all mutual funds/ETFs in reverse order: highest cost basis to lowest cost basis. To get

my total SSA for the upcoming year, I sell "specific shares," meaning I always sell highest-cost shares first to produce the lowest taxable gains.

APPENDICES

- APPENDIX A -
YOUR PLAN WORKSHEET

At the Start of Your Plan . . .

Date of Plan __________ for Spending in Calendar Year __________

Starting Portfolio Value ____________

Investment Portfolio (IP) (95%) ____________ (Off-the-top Reserve = 5%)

Your Multiplier (Your IP/$1 million) ____________

Your Design Choices . . .

- Years for zero probability of depleting = _________
- Initial SSR% = ___.____%. C$ ____ ,___00 per $1 M starting IP.
  SSR% = Safe Spending Rate

  Initial SSA = C$ ___ ,___00/$1 M * Your Multiplier = C$ ____ ,___00/year.
  SSA = Safe Spending Amount
- Plan Investing Cost ≤ __.___%
  Planned net cost deduction from Market Returns

  What is your cost now, before you implement your plan? ___________
- Mix: _____% Stock and _____% Bond

  Weights for Stocks: _____% US and _____% Int'l

  Weights for Bonds: _____% US and _____% Int'l
- What will you do when you recalculate that you have More-Than-Enough?
- List the basic three or four funds that dominate your portfolio:
- Have you set up your accounts to your satisfaction? ________

I file our sheet with our current "Graph of Record." See Chapter 9.

- APPENDIX A -

YOUR PLAN WORKSHEET, CONT'D

Annual Maintanance Tasks

- Month to size up Gifts/Donations by Year End __________
  (e.g., from current year unspent SSA)
- Month end to use for annual return calculations __________
- Following Month
  - First few days
    Calculate Return Rate for last 12 mos.
    Recalculate to see if SSA increases more than inflation.
  - Next week or so
    Sell/rebalance to get MRD into cash from Retirement Accounts.
    Decide on Donations, Tax W/H, and therefore the net to Taxable Account
    Sell/rebalance in Taxable Account to get to SSA net of taxes W/H.
  - Before the end of the month
    SSA for spending upcoming year is all in Money Market/Short Term Bond.
    Adjust autopay amounts that go to your checking account.

History of SSA Calculations

Spending Year	SSA based on $1 M initial IP	Graph of Record SSR%
20 ___		
20 ___		
20 ___		
20 ___		
20 ___		
20 ___		

- APPENDIX B -

OUR (TOM & PATTI) PLAN WORKSHEET

At the Start of Your Plan . . .

Date of Plan Dec 2014 for Spending in Calendar Year 2015

Starting Portfolio Value ______

Investment Portfolio (IP) (95%) ______ (Off-the-top Reserve = ~~5~~ 10%)

Your Multiplier (Your IP/$1 million) ______

Patti more comfortable with 10% than 5% at start.

Your Design Choices . . .

- Years for zero probability of depleting = 19
- Initial SSR% = 4.40%. C$ 44,000 per $1 M starting IP.

  SSR% = Safe Spending Rate

  Initial SSA = C$ 44,000/$1 M * Your Multiplier = C$ ___,__00/year.

  SSA = Safe Spending Amount
- Plan Investing Cost ≤ 0.10%

  Planned net cost deduction from Market Returns

  What is your cost now, before you implement your plan? 0.86%

  ↑ active funds I held
- Mix: 85 % Stock and 15 % Bond

  Weights for Stocks: 70 % US and 30 % Int'l

  Weights for Bonds: 85 % US and 15 % Int'l
- What will you do when you recalculate that you have More-Than-Enough?

  Always "pay ourselves" the SSA calculated. What we don't spend in a year, gift to those we care about before the end of the year.
- List the basic three or four funds that dominate your portfolio:

  S= FSTVX, VXUS

  B= IUSB, BNDX

  cost < 0.07%
- Have you set up your accounts to your satisfaction? Yep. Patti understands and likes the display

I file our sheet with our current "Graph of Record." See Chapter 9.

- APPENDIX B -

OUR (TOM & PATTI) PLAN WORKSHEET, CONT'D

Annual Maintanance Tasks

- Month to size up Gifts/Donations by Year End Oct or early Nov
  (e.g., from current year unspent SSA)
- Month end to use for annual return calculations Nov 30
- Following Month
  - First few days (before Dec 5)
    Calculate Return Rate for last 12 mos.
    Recalculate to see if SSA increases more than inflation.
  - Next week or so (before Dec 15)
    Sell/rebalance to get MRD into cash from Retirement Accounts.
    Decide on Donations, Tax W/H, and therefore the net to Taxable Account
    Sell/rebalance in Taxable Account to get to SSA net of taxes W/H.
  - Before the end of the month (before Dec 20)
    SSA for spending upcoming year is all in Money Market/Short Term Bond.
    Adjust autopay amounts that go to your checking account.

History of SSA Calculations

Spending Year	SSA based on $1 M initial IP	Graph of Record SSR%
2015	$44,000	4.40%
2016	$44,000	4.40%
2017	$46,100	4.60%
2018		
2019		
2020		

- APPENDIX C -

FIRECALC AND VANGUARD RETIREMENT WITHDRAWAL CALCULATORS (RWCS)

We retired folks are acutely aware that we face uncertain future investment returns. The long run historical return rate for stocks is 6.4% real return per year, and it's 2.6% for bonds. The sequence of annual returns is not at all smooth, and the sequence of annual returns we may face has the biggest effect on our chances of depleting a portfolio.

Retirees have experienced periods of many years of zero percent cumulative returns. If we looked at sequences of actual returns for stocks since 1926 (without consideration of withdrawals for spending), we'd find about six sequences (roughly 6%) that were killer starts for a new retiree. I show five of these in this graph C-1.

GRAPH C-1
FOUR 23-YEAR STRINGS OF REAL STOCK RETURNS & 2000 TO PRESENT

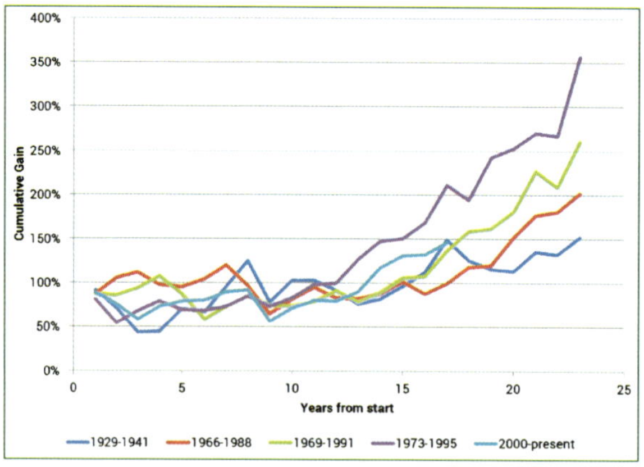

You can see that you would not have been happy to retire in 1929, 1966, 1969, 1973 or 2000. Stocks declined by more than 25% in the first two years for three occasions. Poor returns in the first few years of a retirement period really hurt, because negative return rates are resulting in the biggest dollar decreases.

The drain on a portfolio continued for many years. It took at least twelve years to eventually surpass 0% cumulative real return for stocks for those sequences of returns. It took 17 years for one. These long periods of low cumulative returns means those folks would have seen their nest egg decline most years.

■ ■ ■

RWCs assemble sequences of returns we may face to understand the probability that a spending rate depletes a portfolio. FIRECalc and Vanguard both use historical annual returns for stocks and bonds to construct the possible sequences of returns we may face in the future. They assemble their sequences differently.

FIRECalc uses the sequences of returns as they occurred in the past. For the construction of all the possible sequences of 10-year returns, as an example, FIRECalc will use the actual calendar year returns from 1926-1935, 1927-1936, and so forth. This means the worst sequence is the worst actual 10-year sequence experienced by investors who started their retirement period in 1926, 1927, and so forth. So, "zero probability of not depleting" in FIRECalc means "a portfolio did not deplete even in the worst historical (calendar year) sequence of returns in history."

Vanguard assembles each sequence of returns by randomly ordering historical returns. The first sequence may be the annual returns in order 1984, 1931, 2004, 1927, 1953, and so forth. This method of construction results in many, many trillions of possible sequences. Every time we "run" the Vanguard RWC, it constructs 5,000 sequences that should statistically represent of the total sequences it could construct. This random-order method will construct sequences that are far worse than have ever occurred (e.g., more than 3.5 million 10-year sequences are comprised of just the 10 most negative annual returns!) and far better than have occurred in history. You get a sense of this by looking carefully at the side-by-side graphical displays of the range of ending portfolio values for the same inputs.

I don't think there is a right or wrong method, and we should not be hung up on the small differences in probability of depleting between the two. I personally prefer the FIRECalc method, since I think the actual sequences of return are reflecting returns patterns that changed with changes in inflation as it occurred, efforts government takes to improve our economy in downturns, and the fact that stock returns "revert to the mean;" this means the actual sequences of stock returns are better than would be indicated by random ordering of returns. (See *Stocks for the Long Run* by Jeremy Siegel, Chapter 6, page 93 of the Fifth Edition. A striking conclusion is that for a holding-period of about 17 years, stocks are both greater in return and less variable in annual return rate than bonds. This would not be predicted by the random ordering method.)

You can see that the two RWCs give similar probabilities of depleting for each spending amount. Graph C-2 is 4.50% spending rate ($45,000 C$ spending per $1 million starting portfolio). I used FIRECalc's default assumptions on mix of stocks and bonds. The plot gives a sense of the amount of difference in the year-by-year probability of depleting between FIRECalc and Vanguard.

GRAPH C-2
PROBABILITY OF DEPLETING A PORTFOLIO FROM TWO RWCS

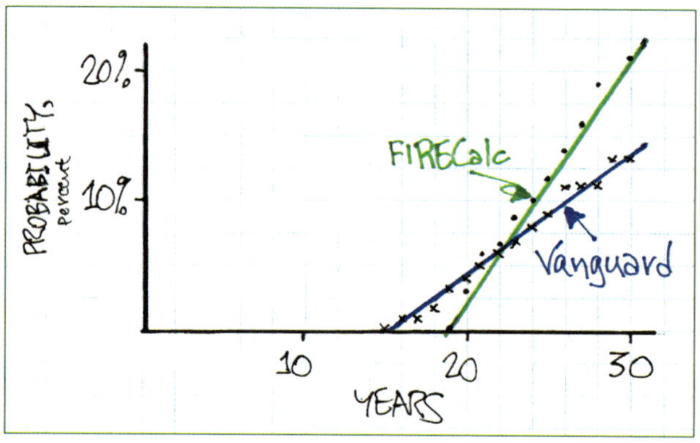

4.50% spending rate at FIRECalc's default mix of 75% stocks

When we plot the data for FIRECalc, the probability of depleting curve looks like a hockey stick lying on a graph. The shaft of the stick equates to many years of zero probability of depleting. There is a clear inflection point (years), and thereafter a rising probability of depleting – the blade angle of the hockey stick.

When we use the Vanguard RWC we get a slight curve to our stick before FIRECalc's clear inflection point. (I may not have captured that initial slow slope in the straight line I drew for Vanguard.) After that, the blade angle for Vanguard is shallower than for FIRECalc.

Vanguard shows a slightly higher probability of failure up to the 22nd year and a lower probability of failure thereafter. If I average the values from years 16 to 30, FIRECalc results in about 25% greater probability of depleting. Therefore, if I use FIRECalc as our workhorse calculator, I think I am being conservative (high on average) on future probabilities of depleting a portfolio. I judge these year-by-year probability differences between FIRECalc and Vanguard as inconsequential in determining our Safe Spending Rate and Amount.

■ ■ ■

RWCs aren't static in the data they use when they assemble sequences: each year they add one more year of data to their store of returns. To a very small degree, the year-by-year probability of depleting a portfolio changes. These very small changes don't alter any of the conclusions we would otherwise derive in our planning. One sees the change from the addition of one more year of data more explicitly in FIRECalc, since one more year of data means you'd see one more sequence of returns for each time horizon on a results graph.

■ ■ ■

The mechanics of FIRECalc. FIRECalc has six key parameters that one can vary: spending, portfolio value, years, investing cost, mix of stocks, and years to use for the data. I always fix two.

1. I always set Portfolio to $1 million on the Start Here Page. That makes it straightforward to find the spending rate.

2. I always set years of data from 1926 (not 1871, FIRECalc's default) on the Your Portfolio page. We want to use 1926 for three reasons.

    a. The Vanguard calculator uses data from 1926. We want to match the years it uses when we check to see if Vanguard's results are consistent with FIRECalc's.

    b. 1926 is a somewhat standard starting point for historical analysis of stock and bond returns. We have the most detail on returns from stocks and bonds from 1926.

    c. That start includes the three worst recessions since 1871, and therefore results in higher probability of failure in future years than if we included data from 1871.

The other four parameters are Spending (I always use constant-dollar spending), Years, Investing Cost ("investing fees" in FIRECalc), and Portfolio Mix of Stocks. To find the effect of changes in one parameter I vary one and hold the other three constant.

For example, to find how the year-by-year probability of depleting a portfolio increases with time, I set the input parameters and increase the years one-by-one. I read the "success rate" on the results page for each year, and I convert that to a probability of depleting as 100% minus the "success rate." I round to the nearest whole percentage point.

■ ■ ■

Information on specific graphs. I labeled or described the inputs for the redrawn displays of two FIRECalc graphs, 2-4 and 9-2 (9-1 is the same as 2-4). You should be able to produce graphs that look like these at the FIRECalc site.

I drew several of graphs of the blade angle of a hockey stick or sticks in Chapters 6 and 8; the discussion focuses on the probability of depleting an investment portfolio. I am assuming in those graphs that a retiree had to use his 5% Reserve and was not able to replace it. That translates to less spending from an Investment Portfolio over a complete retirement period. In effect, the retiree would have played his whole game with a longer stick: longer shaft length means the blade angle begins to rise later and it's also a slightly shallower blade angle. The lower spending resulted in a lower probability of depleting a portfolio in the years "thereafter."

As an example, Patti and I start with SSR% of C$44,000 spending rate per $1 million starting Investment Portfolio. Let's assume a 5% Reserve (although Patti insists on 10% for now). That 5% Reserve translates to more than $50,000 set aside, "out of mind," as a Reserve ($1 million divided by 95% to get to the total = $53,000 Reserve). That +$50,000 is a bit over one year of spending for our calculation.

Over, say, 20 years, if all things go well but we never followed a recalculation to spend more. We'd spend C$880,000 out of our Investment Portfolio (C$44,000 * 20 years). But if we hit a year of "bad variability," we'd tap our $50,000 Reserve. (I implicitly assume that's a C$ amount.) If no Recalculation ever told us we could replenish it, we would actually spend C$830,000 over the period from our Investment Portfolio. The $50,000 less is $2,500 less per year over 20 years, meaning we really averaged C$41,500 from our Investment Portfolio for 20 years. Therefore, a C$41,500 stick determines our probability of depleting a portfolio. For the calculations for graphs 4-1 and 6-1, I rounded and used $2,000 per year less spending – C$42,000 spending.

For graph 8-1 and the discussion of Mary and Alice on page 61) I assumed a $3,000 less spending per year, because that's $50,000 over 16 years. For the discussion of our Graph of Record – 2029 on page 70, I used $4,000 less spending per year, because that's $50,000 over 12 years.

■ ■ ■

A brief history of FIRECalc. FIRECalc is the work of one person, Bill Sholar. Around 1999, Bill stumbled across a community of people on the Internet who were discussing the possibilities of taking early retirement and the risks of depleting one's portfolio. One reference site, called the "Early Retirement Home Page," contained numerous articles and spreadsheets to aid people in exploring these issues. Much of the discussion and tools centered around the concept of "safe withdrawal rates" – how much can one withdraw from a portfolio without depleting it and what were the implications of investment fees, other pension income, and so forth.

With a computer background and some years of experience working with websites, Bill decided to create an interactive website to allow people to test various options, and he spent about 18 months developing the initial version, which he published on the Internet in the Spring of 2001. The name came from an acronym for "Financial Independence-Retire Early"... FIRECalc.

Bill has revised the site significantly about 3 times – maintaining the same core behavior, but adding additional options, such as incorporating multiple pensions that might start and stop at different times during the retirement, allowing for export of spreadsheets, and so forth. Each year, Bill updates the database to include the latest stock market results and makes other modifications as needed.

■ ■ ■

Data sources for Graph C-1
Stock returns: http://pages.stern.nyu.edu/~adamodar/New_Home_Page/datafile/histretSP.html
Inflation to adjust for real returns:
https://inflationdata.com/inflation/inflation_rate/historicalinflation.aspx

- APPENDIX D -

DATA TABLE FOR SAFE SPENDING RATE

Constant-Dollar (C$) means the spending adjusts for inflation to maintain its same purchasing power over time independent of changes to portfolio value.

Use Life Expectancy* (Years) to find your Safe Spending Rate.

Your Safe Spending Rate (SSR%) results in zero probability of failing to be able to make a full withdrawal for spending from your portfolio for at least the life expectancy chosen and roughly 1-in-50 chance of outliving and outspending your portfolio in any year "thereafter."

Spending shown is per $1 million starting Investment Portfolio (95% of your total).

The table assumes you have taken 5% "off the top" as a Reserve. You would tap that Reserve in a year of very poor stock returns with the plan of replenishing it when returns improve.

Safe Spending Rate and Multiplier

Years	C$ Spend/ $1 M start	SSR%	Inverse Multiplier
30	$37,500	3.75%	26.7
29	$37,500	3.75%	26.7
28	$38,000	3.80%	26.3
27	$38,000	3.80%	26.3
26	$39,000	3.90%	25.6
25	$39,500	3.95%	25.3
24	$40,000	4.00%	25.0
23	$40,500	4.05%	24.7
22	$41,500	4.15%	24.1
21	$42,000	4.20%	23.8
20	$43,000	4.30%	23.3
19	$44,000	4.40%	22.7
18	$45,000	4.50%	22.2
17	$46,000	4.60%	21.7
16	$47,500	4.75%	21.1
15	$48,500	4.85%	20.6
14	$50,500	5.05%	19.8
13	$53,000	5.30%	18.9
12	$55,000	5.50%	18.2
11	$58,000	5.80%	17.2
10	$61,500	6.15%	16.3
9	$65,500	6.55%	15.3
8	$71,000	7.10%	14.1
7	$77,500	7.75%	12.9
6	$85,000	8.50%	11.8
5	$96,000	9.60%	10.4
4	$104,000	10.40%	9.6

Patti and Tom in December 2014 at the start of our plan. Patti's life expectancy was 19 years.

* Life Expectancy is simply your life expectancy if you are planning just for you. If you are planning as a couple, Life Expectancy is that of the person with the longest life expectancy.

The SSR% is calculated at 85% mix for stocks and 0.18% investing cost. The SSR% shown ensures zero chance of depleting for ≥ number of years shown and 1-in-50 chance of outliving and outspending a portfolio in the years thereafter; for a number of years, this latter criteria was the governing factor.

You cannot use this table to obtain your SSR% if you are not committed to Investing Costs ≤ 0.18%.

Source: FIRECalc.

- APPENDIX E -

OUR TABLE OF LIVING & DYING PROBABILITIES

Our Table of Living and Dying Probabilities

December 2014

		Ages		Living Probabilities				Dying Probabilities			
Year	December	Tom	Patti	Tom Alive	Patti Alive	At least one Alive	Both Alive	Tom Dead	Patti Dead	At least one Dead	Both Dead
0	2014	70	67	100	100	100	100	0	0	0	0
1	2015	71	68	98	99	100	97	2	1	3	0
2	2016	72	69	95	97	100	92	5	3	8	0
3	2017	73	70	93	96	100	89	7	4	11	0
4	2018	74	71	90	94	99	85	10	6	15	1
5	2019	75	72	87	93	99	81	13	7	19	1
6	2020	76	73	84	91	99	76	16	9	24	1
7	2021	77	74	80	89	98	71	20	11	29	2
8	2022	78	75	76	86	97	65	24	14	35	3
9	2023	79	76	72	84	96	60	28	16	40	4
10	2024	80	77	68	81	94	55	32	19	45	6
11	2025	81	78	64	79	92	51	36	21	49	8
12	2026	82	79	59	76	90	45	41	24	55	10
13	2027	83	80	54	72	87	39	46	28	61	13
14	2028	84	81	50	69	85	35	50	31	66	16
15	2029	85	82	45	66	81	30	55	34	70	19
16	2030	86	83	40	62	77	25	60	38	75	23
17	2031	87	84	35	58	73	20	65	42	80	27
18	2032	88	85	30	54	68	16	70	46	84	32
19	2033	89	86	26	50	63	13	74	50	87	37
20	2034	90	87	21	46	57	10	79	54	90	43
21	2035	91	88	17	41	51	7	83	59	93	49
22	2036	92	89	14	37	46	5	86	63	95	54
23	2037	93	90	11	32	39	4	89	68	96	61
24	2038	94	91	8	28	34	2	92	72	98	66
25	2039	95	92	6	24	29	1	94	76	99	71
26	2040	96	93	5	20	24	1	95	80	99	76
27	2041	97	94	3	17	19	1	97	83	99	81
28	2042	98	95	2	14	16	0	98	86	100	84
29	2043	99	96	2	11	13	0	98	89	100	87
30	2044	100	97	1	9	10	0	99	91	100	90
31	2045	101	98	1	7	8	0	99	93	100	92
32	2046	102	99	0	5	5	0	100	95	100	95
33	2047	103	100	0	4	4	0	100	96	100	96
34	2048	104	101	0	3	3	0	100	97	100	97
35	2049	105	102	0	2	2	0	100	98	100	98

Probability Not Alive = 100 - Probability Alive

Joint Probabilities

Both Dead = Tom Dead * Patti Dead

Both Alive = Tom Alive * Patti Alive

You can find a template for this table at www.nesteggcare.com

At least One Alive = 100 - Probability of Both Dead

At least one Dead = 100 - Probability of Both Alive

Source: Vanguard "Plan for a long retirement"
https://personal.vanguard.com/us/insights/retirement/plan-for-a-long-retirement-tool

Instructions for the template: The table assumes you are planning for two. If you are planning for only one, only columns F and L will be useful.

1. Enter start date of your plan (A3), month (B6), year (B7), your names (C,D6) and ages nearest your start date (C,D7). Add more years (up to 40 max) to the bottom of the table if you like.
2. Use the Vanguard Probability of Living Calculator and enter your names and ages and appropriate sex. Set Time frame = 1 and Calculate.

   Enter the probabilities for Person 1 and Person 2 in F,G16.

   The spreadsheet will calculate other probabilities. Since Vanguard is using fractional probabilities of living for Person 1 and Person 2, the spreadsheet may not exactly agree with Vanguard's probability for At Least One Alive ("Either") in all years.
3. For each subsequent year, increase Time frame by one year and enter probabilities.

As noted in Chapter 3, we found it useful to plot the "playground slide" for "At least one alive" and for "Both Alive."

- APPENDIX F -
CALCULATE YOUR INVESTING COST

You have to calculate it. No one does this for you. This is the template for the spreadsheet I had to use to find my .86% Investing Cost for the actively managed funds that I held.

Fund Ticker Symbol	Col A Value each Fund or ETF	Col B Expense Ratio %	Col C Annual $ Cost (A*B)
AXYYX	34,321	1.00%	343
BXNMX	23,922	0.85%	203
CPRRX			0
DOYGX			0
. . .			0
. . .			0
. . .			0
. . .			0
Total Porfolio	58,243		
Sum Fund Costs			547
Weighted Percentage Cost			0.9%
+ Annual Advisory Fees, percent			
Investing Costs/Total Portfolio			0.9%

You can download this spreadsheet at **www.nesteggcare.com**.

Instructions for the template:

- List all funds and ETFs you own. Insert more rows into the sheet as needed.
- Enter the dollar value of each: Col A.
- Enter Expense Ratio for each: Col B. You can get this from a site like **www.morningstar.com** for each fund (enter the ticker symbol).
- The sheet will multiply value * Expense Ratio to get total $ cost for each: Col C
- The sheet will add the totals for Cols A and C.

- It will divide total for C by total for A. This is your weighted cost of ownership of funds and ETFs as a percentage of total value before any Advisory fees you may incur.
- Add your Advisory fees, if any, typically expressed as a percentage of Asset Under Management (cell F24).
- The sum of the two percentages is your total Investing Cost (%) for your Total Portfolio.

- APPENDIX G -

DISPLAY OF THE POTENTIAL SSR% TO USE IN FUTURE YEARS

This table displays the SSR% – from Appendix D – that Tom and Patti should use when they recalculate in any future year. The SSR% is associated with Patti's Life Expectancy (the longest lived of the two of us). Using the Vanguard calculator, we find her life expectancy does not decline by one year for each added year she lives (highlighted cells). Therefore the SSR% does not increase in all years.

You can download a template from **www.nesteggcare.com**.

	Dec	Patti	Patti's Life Expectancy			CD$ per $1M		
Yrs	Year	Age	Years #	Age	Year	Inv Portfolio	**SSR%**	**Inverse**
Start	2014	67	19	86	2033	$44,000	**4.40%**	**22.7**
1	2015	68	18	86	2033	$45,000	**4.50%**	**22.2**
2	2016	69	17	86	2033	$46,000	**4.60%**	**21.7**
3	2017	70	16	86	2033	$47,500	**4.75%**	**21.1**
4	2018	71	16	87	2034	$47,500	**4.75%**	**21.1**
5	2019	72	15	87	2034	$48,500	**4.85%**	**20.6**
6	2020	73	14	87	2034	$50,500	**5.05%**	**19.8**
7	2021	74	13	87	2034	$53,000	**5.30%**	**18.9**
8	2022	75	13	88	2035	$53,000	**5.30%**	**18.9**
9	2023	76	12	88	2035	$55,000	**5.50%**	**18.2**
10	2024	77	11	88	2035	$58,000	**5.80%**	**17.2**
11	2025	78	10	88	2035	$61,500	**6.15%**	**16.3**
12	2026	79	10	89	2036	$61,500	**6.15%**	**16.3**
13	2027	80	9	89	2036	$65,500	**6.55%**	**15.3**
14	2028	81	8	89	2036	$71,000	**7.10%**	**14.1**
15	2029	82	8	90	2037	$71,000	**7.10%**	**14.1**
16	2030	83	7	90	2037	$77,500	**7.75%**	**12.9**
17	2031	84	7	91	2038	$77,500	**7.75%**	**12.9**
18	2032	85	6	91	2038	$85,000	**8.50%**	**11.8**
19	2033	86	6	92	2039	$85,000	**8.50%**	**11.8**
20	2034	87	5	92	2039	$96,000	**9.60%**	**10.4**
21	2035	88	5	93	2040	$96,000	**9.60%**	**10.4**
22	2036	89	5	94	2041	$96,000	**9.60%**	**10.4**
23	2037	90	4	94	2041	$104,000	**10.40%**	**9.6**

Instructions for the template:

(If you are basing your chart on a female, you will find many rows of your chart will look like ours.)

1. Enter the month start of your plan. (C3)

2. Enter year start of your plan. (C5)

3. Enter name of person who governs SSR% (you or longest lived of if two of you). (D3). Change the names in E3 as appropriate.

4. Enter age of person nearest to the month and year at start of your plan. (D5)

5. Extend the cells to as many years in the future as you like. (extend C28 and D28)

6. Find Life Expectancy (50% value) at the start of your plan for person (C3) from the Vanguard Calculator. Enter correct sex. It's clearer if you use "1" as number of people. (Enter in E5)

7. Add one more year to Current Age in the Calculator and change Time frame to find Life Expectancy. In most cases, you will be lowering Time Frame by one year. But in not all years as described above. Enter the appropriate years Life Expectancy for each year. (Column E.)

8. I chose to highlight the cells where the years of Life Expectancy did not change.

9. From Appendix D, I entered the C$ Spending associated with years of Life Expectancy (Column H); the spreadsheet calculated the SSR%.

You now have a complete chart of the applicable SSR% to use for your Recalculation for many future years. I used the first five years in Appendix H. (You may want to adjust my print area setting.)

- APPENDIX H -

Spreadsheet I Use to Calculate to See If Our SSA Can Increase. Do We Have More-Than-Enough?

The summary table on page 72 extracts data from this table. You get a template of this spreadsheet at **www.nesteggcare.com**. You can also follow along as I recalculate each year in early December at **www.nesteggcare.com**. Once you've set up your sheet, you have to enter only three numbers into the sheet each year: inflation rate in the past year and time-weighted returns for both stocks and bonds. (Time-weighted returns ignore the distorting effect of additions or subtractions to a portfolio.) My key sources for data to input are the inflation (COLA) adjustment from Social Security and the 12-month return rates Fidelity posts for our stocks and bonds within a few days of the end of a month (see display on page 91).

Spreadsheet to see if our SSA can increase by more than inflation. Do we have More-Than-Enough?

Spending Year	**2015**	**2016**	**2017**	**2018**	**2019**	**2020**
Year end Date for Calculation	12/15/14	12/15/15	12/15/16	11/30/17	11/30/18	11/30/19
Inv Portfolio before withdrawal	1,000,000	944,643	1,002,100			
SSA Withdrawal	44,000	44,000	46,100			
Inv Portfolio after withdrawal	956,000	900,643	956,000			
End of Year						
Inflation in Yr (SS % increase)		0.0%	0.3%			
A Inflation Adjust prior SSA		44,000	44,132			
Our Return Pct for last 12 mos.		-1.19%	11.27%			
Current Portfolio prior to withdrawal		944,643	1,002,100			
Applicable SSR%	4.40%	~~4.50%~~	4.60%	4.75%	4.75%	4.85%
Memo: Patti's age nearest calc date	67	68	69	70	71	72
B Calculated potential new SSA		42,509	46,097			
Is B > A?		NO	YES			
SSA for Upcoming Yr	**44,000**	**44,000**	**46,100**			
Memo: Cum inflation factor		1.000	1.003			
Orig SSA inflated		44,000	44,132			
Real change from initial $44k		0.0%	4.5%			
Calculation date		12/15/15	12/15/16	11/30/17	11/30/18	11/30/19
Investment Portfolio Value needed for same real spending		na	959,391			
More-Than-Enough per $1 M starting portfolio		na	42,709			
Total SSA (* our Mulitplier)						
Total Excess (* our Multiplier)						
Return Rate Calculation						
Stocks 12 mo. return		-1.53%	12.72%			
Bonds 12 mo return		0.75%	3.02%			
Total for us @ 85% S and 15% B		-1.19%	11.27%	0.00%	0.00%	0.00%

Instructions for the template:

The spreadsheet you download is set up to calculate for the first two years. When you enter data at the start of your plan, the sheet will start on the calculations for the next years; numbers calculated for cells may look a bit strange, but it will work out as you enter data at the end of each year. For more than two years, you will extend cells to the right (into Col F, etc.).

The Set Up of the spreadsheet (I'd guess this takes 20 minutes.):

1. Enter dates: the year of your first Spending Year (C3); the month-day date for the start of your plan – the one you'll use for the 12-month return rates.

2. Enter your chosen SSR% at the start of your plan and for each future year; see your Appendix G. (Row 14)

3. Correct the cell B15 with "Patti" in it. Enter age nearest to the calculation date for that person. (C15)

4. Correct Cell B36 for your chosen mix of Stocks and Bonds. Reflect that mix in the formula in all the cells in row 36 (copy B36 to the cells to the right).

5. Enter the data for your Multiplier: total portfolio (C43). Change the 5% (B41 and C41) if you picked something other than 5%.

Okay. You are set up. The spreadsheet calculates on the basis of $1 million starting Investment Portfolio, and you apply your multiplier. The spreadsheet assumes you pay out all your SSA in your spending year and save not one dime of it by the end of the year: you've spent it or gifted it.

For your recalculation at the end of your first spending year (I'd guess this takes 20 minutes.): For reference, you can see the results of our recalculation each December for the upcoming year at **www.nesteggcare.com**.

1. Enter inflation (SS COLA) for the past year in Cell D9. The sheet will adjust the current SSA; this is your SSA for the next year unless the recalculation says it can be more.

2. Enter your 12-month return rates for your Stocks and for your Bonds in cells D34 and 35. The sheet will calculate your portfolio return (D12); your portfolio value before the upcoming withdrawal (D13); and your potential new SSA

(D16). That SSA will be more or less than your current SSA after the inflation adjustment.

- ✦ If it is greater, enter the new amount in D19 (I round). You can enter "YES" in D18 and color the text and cell green. I would enter also color the cell D14 as green indicating that this is our new SSR%: in effect, you are now using a new Graph of Record.

- ✦ If it is not greater, enter your current inflation adjusted SSA in D19. You can enter "NO" in D18 and color the text and cell red. I would color the cell D14 as red indicating that I am NOT using a new SSR%. We're sticking with the current Graph of Record.

3. The sheet will also calculate your "More-than-Enough" if you do not increase your SSA. This number will be negative in some years: the annual return in the year was not great enough to justify a greater SSA. My calculation the first year showed I "needed" less than I had and my "more than enough" was a negative number. I ignored that result as discussed in Chapter 9 – sticking with the plan. I entered "na" in cells D26 and D27 to get those numbers out of my mind.

MEET TOM CANFIELD

Tom Canfield made his first investment at age 10 when he purchased five shares of Patterson Dental Supply. As the value of his holdings grew through several corporate acquisitions, he patiently added savings from summer jobs and eventually earned enough to pay for a semester of graduate school. That early experience has been the model for Tom's approach to investing. He's been a saver for as long as he can remember. Because his time horizon for when he needed the invested cash for spending was decades away, he invested solely in stocks, reinvested dividends and rode the inevitable compound growth in value over a long period.

Tom earned an electrical engineering degree from Purdue University and an MBA from Harvard University. He enjoyed considerable success as an entrepreneur — and as a mentor for entrepreneurs. He founded and operated Equity Catalysts LLC and served as president and CEO of The Enterprise Corporation of Pittsburgh, which helped match start-up technology companies with angel investors and other resources. He also was adjunct professor of entrepreneurship at Carnegie Mellon University's Graduate School of Industrial Administration (now the Tepper School of Business).

He has been a partner of Social Venture Partners Pittsburgh since its launch and is a founder of NurturePA, Inc., which supports new parents by promoting infant emotional development and early literacy. He also serves on the board of Propel Schools, and he works with several other nonprofits to help them arrange their displays of financial results so they can see their performance trends more clearly.

Tom and his wife Patti live in Pittsburgh. Determining their Safe Spending Rate, and spending accordingly, allows them to enjoy walking vacations, including a visit to England's Lake District.

Nest Egg Care is Tom's first book.